How Much Did You Love?
What Did You Learn?

by

Alex Jones

Eastern Gate Publishing
P.O. Box 7, Millbrook, Ontario, LOA 1GO

Address inquiries to the publisher:

Eastern Gate Publishing
P.O. Box 7
Millbrook, Ontario L0A 1G0
Canada

Second Printing, 1994

Canadian Cataloguing in Publication Data
Jones, Alex
How Much Did You Love? What Did You Learn?
ISBN 0-9696490-0-2
1. Love.   2. Spiritual Life.   1. Title
BP605.N48J66 1992   291.4   C92-090572-2

Dedication

**To Universal Love
and
To Hopi, a pure channel of love**

ACKNOWLEDGEMENTS

Over the years, many people have reviewed my manuscript and have helped me focus my ideas until the present form of this book emerged. I would like to thank them for their support and their many contributions to this book.

My wife, Karen, for her helpful criticism and continual love and encouragement.

Ann Emerson, who helped with an early version of this book and provided valuable editing and direction. Ann has edited and enhanced the second revised edition of this book.

Jim Johans, my spiritual brother, who offered numerous suggestions and patiently provided editing and encouragement through numerous revisions.

Susan Silverman, who helped with a major revision of the section on Transcending Limitations and offered invaluable ideas and general assistance with writing style and editing.

Steve Silverman, who also helped edit the book and provided technical support.

Carol Ballard, a fellow writer who encouraged me to write from the heart, and offered helpful suggestions in developing the affirmations for the Stages of Life.

TABLE OF CONTENTS

INTRODUCTION 1

SELF LOVE 5
   Appreciation of the Self 5
   Self-love and Positive Thinking 14
   Additional Self-love Principles 22
   Affirmations on Self-love 28
   Meditations on Self-love 30

TRANSCENDING LIMITATIONS 33
   Know Thyself 33
   Stages of Life 43
   Inner Healing 65

LOVING OTHERS 71
   The Universal Plan 71
   Aspects of Love Relationships 74
   Loving and Getting Along with Others . . . 78
   Affirmations for Loving Others 94
   Meditations for Loving Others 95

THE LOVE OF GOD 99
   In Love with Love 99
   God Is the Highest Necessity 104
   How to Cultivate Love for God 107
   Manifestations of Spirit 118
   Affirmations for Loving Our Creator 122
   Meditations for Loving Our Creator 123
   Concluding Remarks 126

INTRODUCTION

All of us have to give up our bodies eventually. This earthly life has been compared to a school, in which we spend time learning lessons. At the termination of our earthly sojourn we are asked to evaluate our life as a whole. In order to pass the necessary exam and qualify for our doctorate from the school of life it may be helpful to know what is required of us.

Numerous individuals who have had a close encounter with death or who have clinically died (i,e., have had heart and respiration cease functioning) and have been revived have shared their experiences. From these documented reports many similarities have been revealed: seeing a vision or impression of the major events of their life passing quickly before them, leaving the physical body and looking down upon it, hearing a roaring sound, traveling through a dark tunnel, seeing a brilliant white light, meeting loved ones who have already passed on, meeting and communicating with an exalted loving and compassionate Being and being told that they must come back.

A number of people who have experienced these near-death states and were revived have also reported that two basic questions were asked of them: "How much did you love?" and "What did you learn?" These questions were asked with loving compassion. There was no judgment or criticism.

This book is based on the two questions: "*How much do we love ourselves, others and our Creator?*" and "*What are we learning to bring us closer to Self-actualization?*"

Throughout the book I refer to God in many different ways. When terms appear such as: our Creator, Universal Love, Supreme Intelligence, Divine Consciousness, or Higher Power; it is to be understood that they all represent the same Infinite Spirit. God is viewed not as a stern old man waiting to

1

punish us and send us to a place of eternal suffering on the slightest pretext, but as Unconditional Love.

In this book, God is understood as neither masculine nor feminine. God, as Love, created both the masculine and the feminine principal as equals, but is beyond both. Because of the limitations of the English language, in order to keep this concept clear, it is sometimes necessary to speak of Spirit beyond creation as "It." When Spirit manifests, It often does so in a personalized form, and can then be referred to in terms of He or She. These personalized manifestations may include the Divine Mother, or a great Spiritual figure such as Jesus Christ, or the Deified Leader of any faith.   Please change the gender or particular manifestations mentioned to suit your natural inclination or beliefs.

The terms "Saint", "master", and "great soul" are used to denote a person who has had direct experience of God. These individuals may be from different religious faiths. We all have the potential to reach this state and are Saints in the making. In this book the attainment of our Divine nature has been called Self-realization where "Self" (capitalized) denotes the soul which is eternal, possessing infinite Divine qualities. The self (not capitalized) signifies the soul identified with limited temporary identifications such as the body, status and material possessions and is commonly referred to as "ego" consciousness.

The Threefold Nature of Love

Love can be experienced and expressed in three ways: loving oneself, loving others, and loving our Creator. These expressions of love are closely related. If we are having difficulties with any one facet we will automatically have difficulties with the other aspects. If we have a problem loving ourselves, we will have problems loving others and loving our Creator. We also cannot completely love ourselves if we find it difficult to love others, because in essence everyone is an extension of ourselves.   We are all made in the image of Universal Love, and if we distance ourselves from our Creator, we are unable to know and fully love ourselves or others.

Methods of Advancement

This book presents several methods to assist us in discovering our own unique essence. The first approach is to deepen our awareness of Universal principles, which help form the attitudes necessary to bring about the conditions for love.   The second is the use of affirmations, and the third approach utilizes guided meditations and visualizations.

From the spiritual counseling work I have done, I am convinced that the biggest disease of mankind is lack of self-love. Ultimately this comes from feeling separated from God - Unconditional Love - which is our true nature.   From becoming too identified with a world of change and forgetting our changeless soul nature. *In essence we are love itself.* We need to embrace this truth and extend this love towards ourselves, to others and to our Creator.

In the old and new Testament the highest laws of life were given as a formula to love. This formula points the way to our ultimate destiny. It shows us not only how to answer these two greatest questions of life but how to live it in our own lives. "Thou shalt love the Lord thy God with all thy heart, and with all thy soul, and with all thy mind, and with all thy strength: this is the first commandment. And the second is like, namely this, Thou shalt love thy neighbor as thyself. There are none other commandment greater than these." Mark 12:30. This was the greatest truth when the prophets of the Old Testament declared it as it was when Jesus reaffirmed it. Truth is eternal and these two golden rules for happiness are still the greatest truth today and will be so two billions years from now.

To fulfil these two commandments it is implied that we need to love ourselves.   In giving us the second commandment, Jesus and the prophets did not mean that we should love others the way most of us love ourselves. Many people have such a poor image of themselves that they would never want to bestow this kind of love on anyone else. I would therefore humbly like to clarify the second commandment by offering a third. "Thou shalt love thyself."

Many people have an extremely difficult time fulfilling this third commandment. It is impossible to give the Creator and our neighbor something we do not already feel ourselves. It is for this reason that I have included a section in this book called, "Transcending Limitations," in which I offer various concepts, affirmations and guided meditations that have been helpful for many in identifying and overcoming difficulties.

Many problems with the giving and receiving of love are deeply rooted, and have their origins in early childhood. Together we will explore the various stages of our development and growth to search out where our capacity to love may have been inhibited.   Once we discover our limitations we can apply the practical tools mentioned above which can be of aid in removing these obstacles. It is my sincere desire that this section of the book will help you to identify blockages so that you can remove them and once again become pure instruments of love.

If limiting beliefs are stubbornly rooted, then I encourage individuals to use the information in this book as a starting point only, and explore other writings and if need be, obtain professional assistance.

Please note that I am predominately a Spiritual writer. I am not a therapist. My offerings in this section are mainly from my research in psychological literature, and from my own work in Spiritual Counseling. It is to be understood that this section is an overview of a vast and complex subject that I feel needs to be explored in greater depth.

SELF LOVE

Appreciation of the Self

There is a saying that "God does not create junk." Supreme Intelligence has created the marvels of creation out of Itself. *We are made in the image of God and can be compared to individual sparks of the One Eternal Flame.* When we are in harmony with this Supreme Intelligence, we experience ourselves and all creation as infinitely beautiful and sacred.

Universal Love is what Spirit is. As divine children, our true nature is love. As we strive to develop ourselves, this inner love unfolds naturally and transforms us into God's image. In time we can begin to manifest all the qualities of the Divine. In essence, we have all the power we need to be dynamic, successful and radiant beings. It is our birthright.

Awareness of our Infinite potential is our destiny. Anything less than full awareness of this is delusion and represents a hypnotic trance of denial. When we come to realize that we truly are made in the image of the Divine, we can then recognize the true Self. As a majestic tree is hidden within a tiny seed, so our Infinite nature is latent within us. Unfortunately, very few of us have known we could achieve this state of Self-realization, and it is therefore considered abnormal and foreign. We are conditioned to shut out this awareness and believe that we are mere mortal beings. Those who have achieved this realization, however, tell us that the attainment of such states is the true purpose of life.

Be Thyself

Each of us has been placed on earth to become the best "me" we can be. Each one of us was created special and unique so that we have the potential to blossom with our own dynamic individuality. Few of us realize that we are unique individuals, created to bring out the abilities and talents that we alone possess. Although we have not been encouraged to realize this we were not placed here to live out somebody else's expectations of us, but instead to develop our own unparalleled essence.

At our center, we are exquisitely beautiful and capable beings. There has never been anyone like us nor will there ever be anyone exactly like us again. No one can love as we love. No one else can create in exactly the same way that we can. No one can be us or replace us, and we are therefore essential to the Universe.

God's will for us is that we realize this and learn to truly love and accept ourselves, so that we can feel a passionate joy in being who we are.

When we can feel this confidence about our own being, then our consciousness becomes a magnet, attracting all good things into our life. Feeling dynamic enough to succeed in whatever we choose to do is in accord with our greater evolution.

Self-sufficiency

When we start to get in touch with our dynamic Self, we begin to feel more and more Self-sufficient. We come to feel anchored in an inner sanctuary of joy and love. Centering ourselves in this fullness within, we will find that outer influences do not have as much effect on us.

We eventually come to the realization that nobody can upset or influence us unless we give them the power to do so. Understanding dawns that nobody can make us unhappy if we have chosen to be happy. No one can make us feel inferior and depressed if we have chosen to love and respect ourselves in all conditions and situations.

Gradually learning that this *Inner Love* is not determined or influenced by the actions or comments of others, we begin to see that no amount of ridicule can dampen it. Sarcasm or abuse has no power to destroy it. Eventually we find that we cannot be manipulated by flattery or guilt that others may use to try to control us.

When we are feeling rooted in the Self, we realize that we are complete in our own love and acceptance, and the affections of others are not essential to our Self-esteem. We appreciate acts of love or affection directed toward us, but we are not controlled or unduly influenced by them. Above all, we do not feel a lack within if these are not forthcoming. Nor do we feel a need to control or please or flatter others in order to receive or maintain favorable attention. In the realization of our own worth and beingness we are more interested in sharing or giving of ourselves than we are in receiving from others.

Knowing that we alone are in charge of our destiny also means that possession of material things does not make us feel we are either better or worse than anyone else. When we realize our true worth, our Self-acceptance and love becomes anchored within, and so is not influenced by possessions or status symbols of the outside world.

Fear Less

When we are Self-confident, limiting fears have less influence in our lives. The more love we feel within, the less fear we will experience. From a position of Self-acceptance and love we are better able to handle any situation that presents itself. In time the realization comes that we have within us all the power and strength we need to accomplish anything our hearts and minds decide we want.

The Universe never gives us more than we can handle. Very often, however, it does offer situations that will move us beyond our comfort zone, stretching our capabilities to the maximum. This expansion can be difficult, and without the right understanding and emotional flexibility, we may well feel overwhelmed.

Our Creator is very personal. God dwells in each of our hearts, guiding us toward our highest purpose, and helping us to grow, always working on our behalf for our ultimate welfare. When we are presented with similar situations over and over again it is a sign that we have not learned the needed lessons, and permanently incorporated them into our consciousness. Universal love is guiding each one of us to unconditional self-acceptance, and the fullness of love and happiness at all times.

A Story of Love

The story of Jonathan Livingston Seagull by Richard Bach is an uplifting and endearing fable about the work of love. Jonathan was convinced as a youth that there was more to the purpose of a seagull's life than fighting for food. He loved to fly, and inwardly felt that this was the purpose of his life. He spent as much time as he could trying to increase his flying ability and speed. Through experimentation with various methods, Jonathan found that he could indeed fly much faster and with much more control than was usual for a seagull.

Jonathan eventually moved on to a higher plane of consciousness and met a teacher who assumed the responsibility for instructing him in perfect flight. Jonathan's Guide gradually taught him the powers of mind.

Jonathan finally learned the art of perfect flight by realizing that creation is a play of the thoughts of the Creator. Seeing himself as an unlimited thought of freedom with no restrictions, Jonathan was able to just think of some distant place and find himself instantly there. He also learned that he was not limited by the dimension of time, and could pass freely between the past, present, and future.

Jonathan's Guide encouraged him to learn perfect Love. The more Jonathan dwelt on Love, the greater became his desire to return to his former flock and show them what he had learned. Love burned in Jonathan's heart to lead his seagull brothers and sisters out of their delusion by showing them their own unlimited potential.

Jonathan returned and attracted some seagulls who were interested in knowing how to increase their flying ability. Since he challenged the limiting rules and ways of the elders, Jonathan also experienced many severe trials and persecutions which he endured for the sake of Love.

The Work of Love in Jonathan's Heart

As a youth, Jonathan had a strong sense of Self-love in his heart. He was determined to achieve his own perfection in the form of perfect flight. In order for Jonathan to discover himself more fully, he had to discipline himself. He had to go through painful self-scrutiny to confront and finally release all the destructive programming and limitations that he had inherited from ordinary seagull mentality. Jonathan struggled passionately with his thoughts, feelings and body in order to weed out limitations that kept him from the highest potential of perfect flight. This is a wonderful parable that teaches a Universal lesson.

God's Will propels us forward in our own Spiritual evolution. This is a great truth that it is helpful to remember when we are struggling with difficulties and trying to develop our potential. When we are striving to be more loving and to improve ourselves, then we have linked our life with our Creator's purpose. We can see from the story that Jonathan's pain in dealing with his limitations and his constant working toward a greater excellence in himself was in accordance with the Cosmic Plan.

Perfecting an Ability

In Jonathan's achievements we have an inspirational example to follow in order to arrive at our own success. We need to choose a natural expression of our inner Self that we believe will enhance our life, and then apply ourselves to manifesting this expression. Jonathan loved to fly, and because he was determined to develop his flying ability to the maximum, he ultimately found his highest perfection. If we are going to find fulfillment, *we need to each follow our own dream and do that which we love.* Choosing anything less than this detracts from our ultimate success wellbeing and happiness.

By developing and perfecting an outer expression, be it art, music, business, cooking, housekeeping or whatever we feel inclined to do, we will eventually bring out our inner Divine qualities. In the confident expression of these abilities we will come to know Self-love.

It is therefore an important first step to take hold of your dream, your special ability or talent and feel the enthusiasm and excitement necessary to follow it and bring it to fulfillment. This dream is probably now sitting on the shelf of your heart, and just needs to be dusted off and polished with your enthusiasm. If there is a right time to do this, it is now. Your evolution is depending on it, as is your happiness and peace of mind.

Hold on to Your Dream

If we can allow ourselves to formulate a dream, then we are well on our way to success. The most crucial step is often deciding what we really want, *independent of everyone else's opinion of what is best for us.* Only we know what will fulfil us. In choosing how to pursue our life's dream, it is important to consider the responsibilities we have already taken on. The tendency for most people is to adopt an all or nothing approach. We may feel we have to give up everything in order to successfully follow a dream, or that we are unable to pursue it because of previous commitments. It is possible to balance duties and desire if we are clear about our intention and can feel the state that we hope to attain by following the dream. It is these positive inner feelings that will bring the true fruits of our yearning and labor. We may wish to learn to fly an airplane because of the tremendous feeling of freedom and expansion it can offer us. With that ultimate purpose in mind it is possible to change the outer form of our desire, if necessary, and still maintain the essence of our dream - in this case the feeling of tremendous freedom.

As an example, during a mid life crisis a business man realized that he had always wanted to be a teacher. He had a business of his own which required a great deal of his time and prevented him from going back to school to retrain himself as he wished to do. Upon reflection he realized that being an inspiration to others was the thing that gave him inner satisfaction and happiness. He enrolled in an evening course on public speaking and began doing lectures on topics about which he had knowledge or that were of interest to him. This ultimately lead to writing a book that became very popular and was an inspiration to many people. In this way the man found fulfillment and deep satisfaction.

Any disciplined effort yields benefits. If, for example, your love is music and you are determined to develop this art, then you will realize that studying its various disciplines requires patience and a keen sense of concentration. As you begin to see your musical ability as well as your patience and ability to concentrate increasing, you will begin to enjoy the process and realize who you are becoming. We begin to love another aspect of ourselves as we see it unfolding. Mastering other expressions of ourselves will likewise expand our awareness and our sense of ourself.

Manifesting Your Heart's Desire

Here is an exercise that can help to clarify your dream and continue to work on it until it becomes a reality. First write down your number one dream on a piece of paper. Now place this paper somewhere where you will see it every day as a reminder of your desire.

Congratulations for being clear about your true desire, and committing it to paper. It is no longer filed away in the drawer of your mind. It is now exposed to the sunlight of your aspirations.

Now find a notebook and label it "My Heart's Desire," or some other title that personally inspires you. Work on two open pages together or divide a page into two. The left side will be used for recording old limiting beliefs and obstacles, and the right side will be for recording new beliefs, resources, and compelling visions that move you forward towards your dream.

On the right side of the page record how much time you can constructively spend on your dream every day, or during certain periods of the week. Also, on the right side of the page, write down all the positive reasons why you absolutely must follow your dream. Add any uplifting or practical thoughts that you have heard or read that will keep you inspired and centered on your heart's desire. Record on the right side all the pain you will experience if you fail to follow through.

On the left side of the page write down any critical thoughts, usual actions, rationalizations or distractions that would cause you to miss your appointment with your dream. To help you overcome these limiting programs, determine the steps necessary to overcome these obstacles, and record these over on the right. You may find yourself going back and forth between the left and right sides of the page as you discover new impediments and then figure out the means to overcome them. Write any of the old negative thoughts that have kept you from moving forward in the past on the left. Then write on the right ways you can surmount the difficulty. Be creative and courageous about this and new solutions will appear.

Work on this notebook for a few minutes every day, and, at the end of the week, read the entire book and see what tendencies and impressions emerge. Do this until you are established in working on ways and means to accomplish your dream.

As you perfect your dream, you will find new strength to pursue it and ways to overcome obstacles and barriers. Your joy will increase as you achieve greater and greater success. When you see your achievements finally manifest, you will begin to experience the reality of your own unlimited potential.

Self-love and Positive Thinking

Living out the Patterns of Our Thoughts.

People tend to underestimate the power of thought. Manifesting in the form of energy patterns, *thoughts are things*: they have substance, and they are very powerful. When we think strongly and repeatedly about a particular subject, the thought pattern creates a field that works like a magnet and draws to us the very thing we are thinking about. This can be extremely positive or most negative depending on the thoughts we dwell upon. We draw to us what we focus on.

If, for example, we think we deserve success and prosperity and act accordingly, then these are the circumstances we will attract into our lives. When we think well of our body, then we will care for it with proper food and exercise, and create a state of good health.

If we are constantly thinking that we are unsuccessful, then we will draw the conditions and situations into our lives that would make us fail. Feeling that we are not good enough can make trouble in many areas. If the thought pattern is strongly entrenched in our subconscious mind that we are unworthy of love and deserving of punishment, then we will probably attract an abusive or a non-supportive friend, associate, boss, mate or relationship.

Most of us do not realize that we create our own destiny by the power of our thoughts and actions. If we take the attitude that whatever conditions we face at any given moment are of our own making and are drawn to us in order to help us grow, then we can use our energy and creativity to find new ways to deal with life's experiences. In this way we will begin to bring about the circumstances we prefer and will then find strength and comfort in following our purpose to the best of our ability.

The Subconscious Mind

We unconsciously act on our accustomed thought patterns and the resultant feelings they create. When we have acted in a certain way enough times we form a habit. From these habits our personalities and characters are formed.

Everything we have thought and experienced is stored in the subconscious mind. If we did not have a subconscious mind, then everything we need to do to carry on a functional life would have to be thought about consciously every time we did anything.

This part of our mind, therefore, works automatically when certain situations arise. If we decide to climb a flight of stairs, we do not have to think about lifting one foot and then the other as we go up. Since we have formed the habit of easily climbing stairs, the sight of them automatically brings into focus all the programming already in place along with the corresponding muscular coordination that gets us up the steps.

A similar process takes place when we look at ourselves in the mirror. The subconscious knows that we have created a certain association with our self-image. As soon as we see the reflection of our face and body in the mirror, the subconscious works automatically to cause us to react either positively or negatively to what we see. If we have been programmed by our parents that we are special and a joy to be seen, then this is what will automatically arise in our thoughts and feelings when we look at ourselves. If we have been conditioned in the reverse, then we automatically become critical and unhappy when we see our reflection. This leads to self-recrimination and often despair from which we may seek solace in pastimes that are destructive to our well being like overeating, or drowning our sorrows.

The Conscious Mind and Free Will

The conscious mind can reason, but the subconscious does not. It responds automatically to the thoughts registered through learned behavioral responses. Most of these were established in childhood when our perspective was limited, and were especially conditioned when something happened with emotiom.

In order to change a pattern, we need to harness the conscious mind and use its powers of reason to decide what we want or do not want in our lives. We have free will and free choice, and can decide what is best for us and what is detrimental. If we are trying to overcome a destructive pattern, then we need to keep thinking and acting in the new way until the subconscious mind is retrained and responds automatically to the new pattern and not to the old. This takes time and persistence, but pays off once our chosen pattern becomes our new habit. It also takes awareness and focus in the moment. Too much of our thinking is off on the past or the future. The present is really all we have and that is where we have power to make desired changes.

Keep on Keeping on

If you have decided to give up smoking, then after meals or at whatever time or with what act the subconscious has been taught to prompt you to light up, you need to plan and to initiate thoughts to change that pattern. Of course at first there is going to be conflict because the conscious mind says not to smoke and the subconscious wants to do so. The body gets used to certain gratifications and wants them.

Usually, in following a new resolution, we are able to succeed the first few times because we feel an initial sense of inspiration and determination. To effect a desired change it is necessary to maintain this determination even when this beginning surge of enthusiasm begins to fade. We need to succeed enough times so that the subconscious mind gets the idea: Non-smoking is now the habit, and smoking is not.

We often get discouraged and do not persist long enough for a new habit to take hold. In this case, we might slip a few times, and then give up and smoke just as much as before. The worst of it is that we then feel like a failure, and allow failure thoughts to overwhelm our minds such as: "I cannot do anything right. I knew I would fail. I am not strong enough." As soon as these negative thoughts are entertained, they start attracting negative situations. Slowly this attitude and these thoughts attract failure to other areas of our life.

Resistant Patterns

In our attempts to remove limiting beliefs, we may find that using will power alone is not sufficient. We may have a sincere desire to change and employ our mind and willpower to do so, but still find ourselves carrying out a particular action in spite of our resolve. Instead of giving ourselves a hard time and feeling guilty, it is more helpful to reflect and to understand why this is happening.

It is useful to assume there was a positive intent, or a reason why this pattern was originally established. At some point in our lives, this pattern was probably precisely what we needed to survive in a specific situation. It might have been a useful response for dealing with early family experiences, or other circumstances. The problem with this is that once a "rule" has been adopted, it is the nature of the subconscious to preserve and use the same survival mechanism even though conditions have changed and that behavior is no longer useful or appropriate and may even be harmful. If we wish to transform or control a habit, we need to understand the reasoning behind our initial responses, determine the benefit we received from that habit, and find a more appropriate way of reacting to the stimulus that prompts it.

For example, we might explore a family situation where a mother finds it difficult to outwardly express her love through words and physical affection. She may find it easier to show her love by preparing wonderful meals for her husband and children. The children will soon learn that food is more than a means to nourish the body, but nourishes the emotions as well. Eating the food obviously pleases the mother. Food then comes to symbolize acceptance and love. The children may then unconsciously begin to believe that the more food they consume, the more they are loved and accepted. The feeling of being heavy and full then represents security, love and acceptance.

In later life, these individuals may decide to diet because of health problems from overeating or a poor bodily image. Feelings of hunger would then unconsciously represent the removal of love and result in painful feelings of deprivation. (Of course the same physical sensations could be interpreted by another individual as lightness and freedom.) To those who associate love with food, an empty stomach is a direct threat to their feelings of security. To use willpower alone would be futile because in essence this person would unconsciously feel that using willpower to disconnect from food is taking away love and security as well. If, however, such a person can realize what was behind this and find another way to feel loved, they would have an easier time in succeeding with their diet.

It is for this reason that the focus of this book is to encourage us to consciously formulate what it is we love and what makes us feel secure and able to express ourselves. In fulfilling our basic need for creative self-expression we will then feel nourished from within. In the expression and discovery of *inner qualities* we begin to love and value ourselves and move away from being dependent upon outer things or others for love and satisfaction.

When a habit is very resistant to change, it is expedient and rewarding to explore earlier conditioning. This will be dealt with more fully in the section on Transcending Limitations.

Review Each Resolve

Sometimes instead of an all-or-nothing approach, it is better to gradually curb a tendency. For habits such as wrong eating, it works better to replace junk foods gradually with good food. Similarly, in beginning a new exercise routine, it may be far better to start off gradually, rather than immediately trying to qualify for the Olympics. For people in certain situations it sometimes is better to simply stop. In the case of a strong, abusive tendency, for example, it is best to make up one's mind to cut the habit off immediately and seek professional help, to make this change possible.

Learning Through Experience

We learn through experience. If we are practical and know that we are going to stumble sometimes, then attempts that miss the mark will not be so devastating. If a baby learning to walk falls, it simply gets up and tries again. We do not consider it a failure because it cannot walk the first or even the hundredth time it tries. In fact we celebrate its attempts and encourage it to carry on.

In our example of Jonathan Livingston Seagull, he experimented again and again in his quest for perfect flight. Many attempts were complete flops. Even when his spirits were down and he seemed to get nowhere, he still carried on. By learning from his mistakes, he finally found the right formula for success.

Life is a learning process right to the very end. Unfortunately most of us were judged or punished for making a mistake. It is important for us to realize that a mistake is merely an indication of something that does not work. If we recognize this and applaud ourselves for our attempts to move forward, then setbacks from isolated incidents are not so daunting. We can maintain an optimistic attitude and move forward as we try new things until we find what does work.

The Diamond Within

Self-love is built from understanding, accepting, and cherishing who we are right here and now. We need to like and enjoy being who we are in spite of our apparent flaws. Each of us has strengths, talents and ability to love. Unfortunately we have been taught to find flaws and weaknesses and not to give ourself credit for our good qualities. What we focus on is what we experience. Focusing on all the good in us helps us to realize that we are lovable.

It is paramount that we become our own best friend. Our imperfections can be compared to a layer of mud covering a beautiful diamond. Once baked on by the sun, the mud appears to be a permanent part of the diamond. In reality, we know from experience that it can be removed with work.

Like the diamond, our essence is hidden by the mud of what we consider to be our personality flaws. Flaws are not our permanent reality; they are just misconceptions that we have been programmed to believe. With the right under-standing and effort these, too, can be permanently removed and our innate beauty and lovableness can come out of hiding.

Our conditioning taught us to put ourselves down. Suppose there are three large specks masking twenty percent of a diamond, leaving eighty percent of the diamond clear and radiant. If someone found the diamond, they would sing in their heart and celebrate its beauty. Cherishing it, they would wash or rub the specks away. Most of us do not do this with our special and unique beingness. We become so preoccupied with the twenty percent flaws that we consider them to be one hundred percent of who we are, compare ourselves to others whom we suppose to be more talented or together, and feel inferior. We may become defensive and stubborn about our imperfections, believing they are an essential part of us. When we feel helpless or unwilling to change, we find it difficult to feel good about ourselves. We then consider that our company is probably undesirable and end up doing anything we can to escape from ourselves which may even isolate us from others.

When we make the decision to accept and enjoy being who we are in the present, what we consider to be flaws then become something we can decide to change or remove, not things that possess us and make us dislike ourselves. Once we have understood this, we can enjoy the process of becoming all that we can be.

Love Yourself No Matter What

Above all, we need to learn to love ourselves even if we are not 100% consistent in keeping our good intentions. From my early upbringing I coined a phase for myself: "The second mistake is worse than the first." For example, having decided one day on impulse to diet, I might severely overindulge. If I had simply noted that I had acted against my resolve, and set my intentions to do better next time, then I would have benefitted and have used my conscience as it was intended. But my tendency then was to get discouraged and beat myself up with guilt. That only ended up in my going out and bingeing even more. Under the influence of guilt, we tend to project onto others the anger we feel for ourselves. Then, "The second mistake truly is worse than the first."

If we have the faith that we are continuously growing, then we can love and accept ourselves even when we feel blocked and don't seem to be making much progress.

Suppose we decide we want to perfect our abilities through working on some creative endeavor such as a painting or writing a book. At times during the creation of this work we may well find ourselves stuck. Perhaps we feel a lack of inspiration and nothing seems to gel. If we have done some homework, we can look at this as a growing experience. Perhaps we need to restructure the work, or take a fresh perspective. Maybe we need to stop working on the project for a short time so that new and vital information can come into our thinking. Then we can go on with renewed inspiration rather than letting ourselves wallow in doubt and self-recrimination.

Once we have embarked on the road to transcendence, it is necessary to keep our goal constantly before us. In this process we can view obstacles as opportunities designed to increase our strength and determination and, in the long run, our self-esteem.

Additional Self-love Principles

Balance in Body, Mind and Soul

Each of us is a threefold being, having a body, a mind, and a soul. To be ideally happy and charged with Self-confidence, we need to learn to balance them all. Physically we can look after our health and appearance. Materially we can learn to attract all we need in order to have a full and prosperous life. Emotionally we can examine, use and expand the range of our feelings and give attention to our relationships with others. We can develop our minds and come to realize that everything that happens to us is a result of our own thoughts and actions arising now or traceable to some thought pattern or conditioning from the past. Spiritually we can find our oneness with our Creator.

To have a beautiful and well-cared-for body, but be devoid of Spiritual understanding is to demonstrate a limited sense of who we are. To have a well-developed intellect, and yet be out of touch with our feelings, limits our enjoyment of life and our ability to relate meaningfully to others. To have high

Spiritual aspirations and to live in poverty is not the ideal either. To attain balance in all of these areas leads to true happiness and Self-love.

Happiness in the Here and Now

If we believe that we cannot achieve happiness until we have achieved perfection, then we will be unhappy for most of our existence. The road to self-discovery can be long and trying. We need to accept and love ourselves where we are right now, and at every point along the road of life. This is the strategy that brings contentment and pleasure. Inner happiness and Self-love work hand in hand. We cannot have one without the other. As souls, we are, in essence, perfect. Happiness comes from the understanding that no matter what seems to obscure it, we are that essence. If we are able to be cheerful and optimistic under all circumstances and situations that come in life, then we will find ourselves manifesting this state.

Changelessness is an attribute of God. Changeless, never-ending, unconditional Joy is an aspect of Spirit. When we can smile under all fluctuating changes in a world of relativity, then we are beginning to live what is our changeless, perfect, and joyous nature. If we can hold on to our self-love when everything around us is trying to tear it down, then we are beginning to become one with Changeless, Unconditional, Universal Love.

We have the absolute right and responsibility to love ourselves now. Anything that seems to undermine our Self-love and respect is not only destructive, but out of harmony with God's will and higher purpose, counter to the laws of the universe, and need not be taken seriously.

Living in the Present

Living in the now is the essential formula for Self-love. If we are totally living in the present, then we will not need to be overwhelmed with guilt for past mistakes and failures. The past is history. The only thing we can change is our present attitude and whatever meaning we choose to assign to any historical event. We only have the ability to bring about change where we are right now. Anxieties and fears about what might happen in the future are debilitating, and stand in the way of using the opportunities we have in the present moment.

The past cannot be changed, nor can the future be realized until it becomes the present. If we are living too much in the past or future then we are not focused on the present, which is the one thing that we can control and make use of. We do not have the power to change the past. *The only power we have is in what is going on right now.* So long as we are doing our best, we can feel good about ourselves without reference to past and we are laying the right foundation for the future. The more positive and constructive we are in the present the better the future we will experience.

This way of being brings us life and vitality. We are free to concentrate fully on what is going on now. We can enjoy life because we are centered in the reality of the present moment unhampered by guilt or fear. We develop an appreciation for the wonders of creation and this leads us to feel united with the glory of God.

Principles of Affirmations

Affirmations are statements of truth. The subconscious mind respects both the spoken and written word. It has been programmed by all the thoughts and words we have put into it with emotion and feeling over the years. By repeatedly saying and writing an affirmation, the subconscious mind can learn to accept and act on new and more effective patterns. *Impregnating the subconscious mind with positive thought patterns forms an energy field that draws the object of the affirmation to itself.* However, we have to remember how long a time present attitudes, beliefs, and feelings have been held and acted upon. In order to change an entrenched pattern one has to persist long enough to supplant the ways we have been used to responding.

When affirming for a particular result, we need to free ourselves from any thoughts that are in conflict with our purpose. Contrary, negative thoughts and beliefs that arise need to be promptly noticed and dismissed. To fight with them in an effort to get rid of them will cause them to become an obsession and to be more firmly entrenched. Simply concentrate fully on your chosen affirmation. Sometimes it helps to take two sheets of paper (or draw a line down the middle of a sheet). On the right side write the affirmation. On the left, write down any negative thought that arises. Write the affirmation again on the right and again the negative on the left. Persist with this until the negatives no longer arise. You do not fight the negatives; you acknowledge them and return to the one you wish to implant. This clears the way for the affirmation to do its work.

If we place our attention on the repeated affirmation, then it will in time establish itself in our subconscious and materialize in our life. Affirmations are in accord with universal laws. If our concentration is deep and sincere enough, the law will be fulfilled and the result will be forthcoming.

When affirming, the following points should be kept in mind:

- Affirmations need to be intellectually understood and emotionally felt.

- Affirmations must always be stated positively. Never say I will not do something. The mind needs things positively stated.

- Note that whatever follows "I am" has a great power. Be careful never to follow it with a negative.

- If an affirmation runs contrary to what you feel to be true, then ease into it by saying "I am becoming more...

- Concentration on a thought produces a field of energy which draws to itself the object of that concentration.

- Affirmations should be repeated many times: first out loud, then whispered, and finally thought of mentally until the subconscious is impregnated with its vibration. Writing affirmations is most useful in establishing a new pattern and reinforces and makes the spoken one more effective.

- Affirmations are best practiced just before going to bed and upon waking in the morning, since at these times we are closest to our subconscious self.

- Assume whatever position is comfortable, with the spine straight and relaxed and the mind alert.

- Close your eyes and repeat aloud or mentally, the thought you want to implant in your subconscious mind.

- Repeat the affirmation throughout the day whenever possible. This strengthens its impression on the subconscious.

- Visualize what is affirmed, as if it were already your present reality.

- Let go of contrary thoughts and beliefs. Rise above them. If any come up, just go on concentrating on and repeating your chosen affirmation.

- Be gentle and patient with yourself, maintaining a joyous sense of becoming.

- Realize that what you are affirming is your birthright.

- It is most advantageous if you use your chosen affirmation for at least 21 days so that it becomes firmly established. Some feel that forty days is an effective span for a stubborn pattern.

Reclaiming Our Dignity in the Present Moment

Instead of limited thinking, we need to begin thinking expansively. We need to turn self-destructive thinking around and think the truth: "I am love," "I am worthy and lovable right here and now." If we continually tell ourselves that we are trying to become or do something, then we are programming ourselves for what might happen sometime in the future. However, since the future is always in the future and not in our present, it may never happen. Each time we think in this manner we project our desire into the unknown, and so put it into a questionable place.

We need to believe that we already own the desired result in the present moment, and that it only needs to be rediscovered or reclaimed. If we think and believe strongly enough that we are lovable, then it will become so. We need to repeat to ourselves affirmations such as, "I am lovable and all good things are mine," instead of, "I will become lovable and all good things will come to me." We need to claim our birthright in the present tense as something we already possess. This is what convinces the subconscious. Sometimes it is useful to affirm the process of growth and change, as in repeating "I am becoming the person I always wanted to be."

We need to reclaim our infinite potential with authority. We need to demand from the Universe our rightful share of its treasures. Everything we need or could want is here in the unmanifest state. The Universe is set up to give us what we ask for and believe we deserve. We have free will and God does not interfere with that. If we passively beg for something and are filled with doubt, we will receive little. With this attitude we cut ourselves off from what could be ours and limit our ability to receive.

Most of us do not understand that we have been given the power and conviction of mind to manifest our potential instantaneously. Our minds need to be trained to rediscover our innate beauty, worth and ability to have what we need and desire. We have to believe that this potential is already within ourselves, rather than coming from some outside source at some time in the future. Believing that we possess this ability to manifest now allows our supreme nature to start to blossom in the present, even though it may unfold gradually.

Affirmations on Self-love

- I am a child of the Universe and share in all its bounty.

- I am a unique expression of God's love, joy and abundance.

- I am created in the image of Divine Love.

- I love myself as God loves me - unconditionally.

- I am a spark of the Divine Flame.

- In my essence I am Godlike. I am sacred and inwardly beautiful.

- Loving and being loved is my natural state of being.

- Love abides in me.

- I am worthy of God's bounty and love.

- I am a child of God, and complete within myself.

- I choose to love myself under all conditions.

- I cherish myself. I love and enjoy being me.

- Today I decorate myself with jewels of self-acceptance and love.

- I am filled with joy and gratitude for all the good that I experience.

- I am at peace, in harmony with All That Is.

- I am becoming the person I always wanted to be.

- God's will for me is unconditional happiness and fulfillment.

- I choose to love myself today and every day.

- I am lovable.

- I am unique and special just as I am

- Each day I am happier, more prosperous and more loving.

Guided Meditations

This book offers guided meditations to help you unite with your true essence. It provides descriptions of a scene or a mental exercise, so that you can visualize the experience as if it were actually happening. It is most powerful if you not only picture things visually, but also inwardly hear the sounds and feel the various emotions and sensations that go with it. Your subconscious accepts these as real, and by this method what is visualized and thus experienced is attracted to you and will come into being as part of your reality.

Some people have trouble visualizing. If you cannot create an image in your mind but you can create the sounds or the physical feelings of an experience, emphasize these modes of perception instead. They are equally effective. You can also talk to yourself or tell yourself a story as if you were reading it from a book. Some people visualize by remembering how something looks, or hear it by remembering the sound.

Meditations on Self-love

Exercise 1

Close your eyes and see your own image. As you hold this picture of yourself in your mind, repeat your name several times. Repeat your name with love, reverence and awe.

Continue to visualize yourself and reflect on one or more of these truths . Address them to yourself. "I exist." "I am alive, a reality of the cosmos." "I am me, nobody else can be me." "I am special and unique." "I was born to be me."

Now gaze into a mirror and look yourself straight in the eyes, and with love repeat your name several times. With dignity and respect, realize whose presence you are in. Accept that you are the handiwork of Supreme Intelligence. Tell the reflection you see in the mirror, "I am happy to be me. I accept and love myself. I am exceptional in my own special way."

Do this daily upon rising and before going to bed. Repeat this until you truly feel it is special to be you.

Exercise 2

Close your eyes and see yourself as a brightly shining star. See how necessary your light is to the brilliance of the Cosmos and how the Universe would be incomplete if your star were removed.

Now realize that in reality nothing can be removed from the Cosmos, for it is the all in all. You can change form but can never be annihilated. Repeat, "I am essential to the Universe. The Cosmos needs me. It is incomplete without me."

Look into a mirror and repeat with conviction the affirmation, "I am essential to Universal well being. The Cosmos needs me. It is incomplete without me. I am needed just as I am"

Exercise 3

Close your eyes and get a sense of your body. Now get a sense of your mind. Feel that you have a body and mind that work together to carry out the various functions of life.

Now let go the thought of your body. Feel that you are mind only. Realize that you could still exist even if you did not have a body.

Now create and wear a totally different body. See yourself in this new body living in another shining reality. See your smiling radiance.

Repeat the following affirmation, "I will never cease to exist. Nothing can destroy me. I will live forever. There is no end for me."

Now look in a mirror and repeat to yourself. "I will never cease to exist. Nothing can destroy me. I will live forever. There is no end for me."

Exercise 4

Visualize your Creator as a glorious White Light. See yourself coming out of the Light. The Creator has just formed your being and placed you in creation.

See a ray of light and love connecting you to the White Light. See this Light glowing within you. See that you are always connected to and loved by your Creator.

Exercise 5

Visualize your Creator in whatever form is special to you. See that in essence you are exactly the same as this image. Now see your Creator sharing all things with you. Know yourself as Universal Love, Wisdom, Joy, Peace and Abundance.

Exercise 6

Feel relaxed and peaceful. Visualize your life's dream. Choose someone as a role model who has already accomplished something similar to your dream, and watch him or her actually performing or manifesting it. Now mentally take that person's place. See yourself accomplishing your life's dream with ease and grace, in your own unique way. Enjoy the accomplishment.

TRANSCENDING LIMITATIONS

Know Thyself

The premise of this book, as defined in the first section, is that we are made in the image of God, and in essence contain all the qualities of the Divine within ourselves. These qualities are already ours. When we become aware and attain deeper states of consciousness, we can experience them as our permanent conscious reality. For this purpose it is suggested that we find and work with one or more of our special talents and develop them.

We have already compared our inner being to a diamond which may be temporarily covered with the mud of imperfections. We have been created as diamond-like personalities, and must take responsibility to clear ourselves of any encrustation with the help of our own uniqueness and in partnership with the Creator.

Through the spiritual work of deep prayer and meditation we can eventually overcome barriers, but it is usually our personal blocks and lack of self love that prevent us from going deep within and finding the healing we seek. Therefore, in addition to practicing Spiritual disciplines, the goal of this section of the book is to help us reclaim our true nature through becoming aware of self-limiting beliefs, releasing the pent-up feelings involved with them, and letting them go.

Blocks to Joy

Most families teach their children that too much fun and spontaneity is somehow wrong. In fact, the expression of any strong emotion is generally discouraged in most homes, schools, and churches. Children usually are not encouraged to be exuberantly happy, full of energy and laughing with excitement. Instead, they are hushed up and told to "be quiet and keep in line."

The simple truth is that *when we suppress our natural joy, we also separate ourselves from our Creator.* God is joy, and when we are happy and spontaneously expressing our own inner life, we are in harmony with our Higher Power.

Many great souls have told of their indescribable joy when feeling connected with Spirit. They spontaneously sang of their love for God wherever they were, and to whomever they met. Saint Francis could not contain his joy, and sang his praises to all creation: to the birds, the wind, brother sun and sister moon.

Joyous Affirmations

- As a child of God, I am worthy of happiness.

- The sun of joy illumines my life.

- I share my Creator's joy in my life.

- I find joy in everything I do.

- Today I will take time to enjoy and celebrate all the good things I have.

- I choose to live in peace and joy.

- The door of my heart is always open to joy.

- I am happy now.

- Today is the best day of my life.

- Today I am wearing a billion-dollar smile.

- God is the Joy that I seek.

Meditation for Happiness

Close your eyes and search your memory for a time in your life in which you felt extremely happy. See yourself smiling and radiating joy. Recreate the circumstances - any sights, sounds, smells, or sensations that might have been present. Recapture that joyous feeling, and find a phrase which best expresses and intensifies it. Repeat that phrase over and over in your mind as you continue to feel your expanding joy.

Now open your eyes and slowly look around you. Keep repeating your chosen phrase and allow yourself to carry that feeling of joy into your present situation. Continue to move back and forth from the past happy scene into the present until you can hold that inner joy throughout the day. Keep this picture and feeling so that you can call it up whenever you need it.

Original Pain of Separation

When we came into in this world we lost the conscious awareness of our oneness with our Creator. *In this separation we do not know our true essence and all the divine qualities we possess.* We often experience a state of pain and insecurity as a result of being separated from our true Self. In our attempts to remove this pain and feel complete again we usually focus all our attention outside ourselves. We attempt to create a state of permanence and security in the world. This can never work for this imperfect world is constantly in a state of instability and change. At best it offers only temporary pleasures and fleeting satisfactions. Our futile attempts to achieve wholeness by the outward means of trying to appease our senses and desires ultimately results in frustration and annoyance causing our pain to become even more acute. Yet ultimately pain and suffering can be our salvation if it forces us to look within and rediscover our true nature.

This separation from our God nature sets us up to be neurotic. *When we are born we feel a disconnection from the only true Source of Unconditional Love and security. Being totally dependent upon our parents we turn trustingly to them to fulfil our need for this love. No matter how well-meaning our parents are they can never compensate for the original pain of separation from God.* The degree to which our parents are able to channel God's Unconditional Love determines the state of our self-esteem and emotional and spiritual health. In their human condition, however, and because they did not have their needs met, our parents eventually fail to provide us with perfect love and security. In fact our society seems geared to doing just the opposite. When we do not get the love we need from our parents it leads to feelings of unworthiness, rejection and low self-esteem. We then desperately seek this love and reassurance from others.

Most parents, due to their own internal conflicts, not only fail to offer unconditional love, but even fail to satisfy some of the most basic physical and emotional needs of their children. When this happens our pain, fear, and resulting anger and anxiety becomes intensified. The tendency then is to repress these feelings. But these repressed feelings do not go away. They come up in the form of deep anxiety and unhappiness which causes us to use other strategies and to develop characteristics that still do not bring us what we want or need, often doing just the opposite.

Early Programming

Emotional programming begins with our early family and environment, which can include parents, peers, teachers, authority figures, the media, books, and the prevailing beliefs of society as a whole. It has been said that our basic personalities have already been established by the age of three. We are also born with our own unique tendencies which influence the way we respond to early experiences. Different children respond to neglect or trauma in different ways.

Some of this early programming is beneficial and some is not. If as a result we have problems loving ourselves and feeling worthy to connect to Universal Love and Wisdom, we will desperately need to set up new patterns that help reconnect us with our true Self.

Social Influence

Society subjects its inhabitants to mass mental conditioning which makes it difficult for individuals to explore ideas that are not acceptable to the popular culture. For example, we are still ignorant of many of the laws of physics. New natural laws are being discovered all the time, yet these laws have always existed. Every law that will ever be discovered exists now. Some people consider, for example, that the story of Jesus Christ walking on water is a miracle, or perhaps a scriptural mistake. Perhaps Jesus understood unknown subtle laws of nature, as yet undiscovered by our scientists, but accessible to those who have achieved oneness with Universal Wisdom.

Just as society may not be aware of many natural laws, some cultures may teach principles which actively serve to keep people in ignorance. For example, certain *unspoken beliefs* separate people from their inner perceptions. Beliefs such as, "Men should not cry" and, "A woman's place is in the home" are limiting. Many people are taught that expressing strong feelings or high self-esteem is selfish and unacceptable. These beliefs and the feelings that go with them are harmful because they inhibit self-awareness and self-expression, and enjoyment of life.

Parental Influence

Modern psychology has now come to realize that one of the most crucial functions parents must perform is to nourish their children's self-esteem. Children need to be loved and guided in such a manner that they feel secure and confident about their own beingness and their relationship to the world. In this way they attain the confidence and courage necessary for a successful life. Unfortunately the prevailing beliefs about child raising have inculcated the exact opposite.

If we have healthy self-esteem, we can recognize and trust our inner feelings and perceptions. We can express what we feel in a spontaneous and appropriate manner. If children are not properly nourished in these areas, they seldom experience their innate worth and beauty, and so cannot discover and make use of their talents and abilities.

In order for Self-love to grow, we also need gentle guidance, through which we learn to live in accordance with universal principles. Awareness of the inescapability of Divine law causes us to develop a respect for the Universe, and to bring our actions into harmony with that law. We learn that what we put out comes back to us and that we are responsible for the consequences of our actions. Happiness and Self-love blossom when we are at peace with ourselves and the world.

We must also learn self-discipline to reach our goals in life. Children need to be guided and to be given reasonable responsibilities. They need to be shown how to work with concentration and efficiency. This can only be learned through encouragement and praise in order to motivate them to bring tasks to successful completion. *When tasks are performed so that achievement results, self-confidence is enhanced.*

If children receive love without guidance and firmness, they are likely to develop self-centered attitudes, which tend to gives rise to a selfish and moody personality. On the other hand, strict discipline without love creates fear, lack of spontaneity, and serious control issues. By providing a balance of encouragement and gentle, loving, discipline, parents can help their children to develop healthy self-esteem.

Role Models

We gain a sense of ourselves from our parents' expressions and actions. If they treasure us as gifts from the Universe, then we will feel valuable. If we are reprimanded as children for having sad, angry, or sexual feelings, then we are likely to feel guilty every time we have these feelings as adults.

Parents are role models, and children imitate them. For example, a father who is unsure of himself may try to mask his feelings of insecurity by dominating his wife. His son, seeing this behavior, is likely to fail to develop respect for his mother, and for women in general. A daughter in this family might expect to be mistreated by men, and unconsciously attract this kind of man to her when she grows up.

When Mom and Dad do not fulfil each others' emotional needs, they may turn to their children instead. As children, we are unconsciously very astute at sensing needs that are not being met. In our desire to be loved and accepted, we try to fulfil them even though there is no healthy way we can do so. We soon learn that by playing certain roles, we receive attention and approval (conditional love). These roles are often so strongly conditioned that once we have internalized them, we tend to continue to play them throughout our life. It is difficult for us to be ourselves and grow up normally if we feel we can only be accepted if we cater to our parents' needs.

If, for example, a husband does not receive the love and attention he requires from his wife, he may seek it from his daughter and treat her as his "Little Princess." This can cause emotional problems for the daughter as well as creating jealousy and resentments within the family.

If the parents praise the child only for making "A's" in school and showing other signs of mental superiority, it is likely to believe that intelligence is the most important quality, and fail to develop other aspects of its personality. A natural talent in an area such as art or music, when it is not valued by parents, can be neglected or even actively discouraged. The child may then later find it has deep regrets for not having developed this ability.

If we are conditioned to only value certain facets of our being, our sense of identity becomes distorted. Regrettably, we may never have the opportunity or encouragement to become the person we could be. If our uniqueness is squelched, we may grow up to become what Daddy was, or wanted us to be, when our talents might have led us to become something quite different and certainly more fulfilling for us. Many people go to their graves living out the roles and wishes of their parents and never find out who they really were, or what they really wanted, always feeling unsatisfied.

If the conditions in our childhood were not favorable, we may vow never to allow them to happen to us again or to inflict them upon our own children. In our attempt to be different than our parents we may swing to the opposite extreme. Either way we are not free.

For example, if we were subjected to severe control we may give ourselves and our children unlimited freedom. This can produce problems that can be just as hard for the child to adjust to later. When we reach a healthy degree of emotional maturity we can avoid going to extremes by adopting the best from our childhood and releasing the rest. We can realize that we do not have to totally accept or reject the attitudes of our parents.

Take some time to analyze yourself to see if you have adopted any tendencies during your childhood that affect your self-esteem. Write down those that empower you as well as the ones you would like to change. Inner healing is achieved when we can develop our life-enriching tendencies and transform the limiting ones. When you are in touch with your own personal issues and what needs to be done for you, then you can create your own affirmations and visualizations.

These-inner directed exercises can then be adopted from or strengthened by the ones offered in this book.

Unless we make a conscious effort to change, we are likely to perpetuate the limiting patterns we learned in our childhood, and so never develop our talents or reach our potential. One clue to issues that may have their origins in the past is any overreaction to present situations. We may find ourselves becoming irritable or angry over some small inconvenience, or severely depressed over a minor disappointment. These are good indicators of basic patterns we need to examine. We may also find that we are extremely defensive over mild criticism and easily hurt. That is a good sign that the present situation has triggered a response to something painful in our past. Intense emotional responses may surface now that were appropriate, or even crucial then for our survival, but are no longer useful, and probably complicate our relationships now and cause us pain.

For example, a secretary was painfully aware of extreme sensitivity to the slightest rebuke from her boss. She became so paralyzed by any criticism of her work that it was questionable whether she could maintain her position in the company. Through therapy she came to realize that her feelings of shame and rejection were a result of her father's severe reprimands for her slightest errors. As a result of this abuse she grew up feeling very insecure. She realized that her father and the emotions she felt towards him, had become transferred to the criticism of her boss. Learning this, she was able to understand and work through her painful feelings and adopt a healthier response to her boss's corrections.

It is extremely important that we recognize that these inner wounds come from real issues from the past. When we can recognize and accept these for what they were, we can retrain ourselves to have feelings about them that are appropriate now. Many of the strong feelings that are affecting us now were natural responses to difficult situations in childhood. The more we can talk about these issues in a safe environment and express our feelings about them, the easier it will be to resolve them and minimize their effects in the present. We can then find ways to restore peace and harmony to our life, repair whatever damage has been done and fill our unmet needs. When we can accomplish this we can then accept our younger selves with understanding and compassion which is a necessary stage in letting go of guilt and finding healing and growth. Thus we learn to recognize, value and nurture our own "inner child", so that we no longer react defensively or with fear to outside triggers.

Stages of Life

It has become apparent that children go through various stages in their development and that skills and concepts are acquired in a specific sequence. If these developmental stages are interrupted or distorted, it becomes very difficult for the child to acquire these skills later on, although it can be done. Indeed, this comprises most of what we call psychotherapy or inner work.

The following pages outline the various stages of life and offer affirmations and visualizations to help us to reclaim any of the qualities which may not have become properly developed in the years which we were growing up.

The First Year of Life

The first year is the time we normally learn to *trust*. When our needs are met consistently and lovingly, trust is developed. Specifically, parents need to nourish their children by providing food, safety, warmth, and affection. Very often these basic needs are not adequately met. For example, at one time pediatricians believed that babies should be fed strictly on schedule. A mother who accepted this theory might have fed her child every four hours, even though the child may have been crying with hunger after two hours. Even today, it is a common practice to feed babies mechanically, with a propped-up bottle, instead of holding and cuddling them to make them feel safe and secure. Problems arise because very young children feel abandoned when they are left alone in their crib for long periods of time, especially when their crying brings no help.

Parents not only physically abandon children, but can abandon them emotionally as well. By not affirming a child's expression of emotions, the child will become confused about the validity of his own feelings. If parents withhold their affection, children are not sure they are loved or are lovable.

If we do not receive loving attention from our parents, we are likely to question our own worth. We will then doubt that other people or God can love us for ourselves. Although on the deepest level of our being we crave closeness, we become emotionally scarred by not having experienced it at the stage when it was most needed. We then tend to fear being hurt again, and become incapable of recognizing or accepting true intimacy even when it is offered by others. We may fear others will find out how unworthy or flawed we are and so push them away.

Transcending Limitations with Affirmations

One way to heal emotional wounds from childhood is, again, through the use of affirmations. This is a method of self-programming, consciously choosing to replace self-defeating thought patterns. All of us habitually talk to ourselves in some form of inner dialogue. Often this dialogue consists of messages we received, either consciously or subconsciously, from our parents, reflecting their beliefs about us and life in general. There are also unspoken admonitions that children feel and internalize. These are usually negative messages we have accepted which we repeat to ourselves. They act as unconscious affirmations and greatly effect our emotional health.

If children are constantly told that they are bad, their subconscious mind will be programmed with this belief. They may then become depressed and feel hopeless without even knowing why. These inner voices are especially likely to be troublesome when a person is alone and quiet. This is the very reason why so many people find it difficult to be alone with themselves.

Consciously chosen affirmations can gradually replace these limiting voices with powerfully affirming and inspiring thoughts.

Affirmations for the First Year

- My heart is connected to the hearts of my parents though the cord of unconditional love.

- I feel safe and warm in my mother's and father's protecting arms.

- I am cuddled in tender love.

- I have everything I need. I am totally cared for.

- I feel comfortable and serene, wrapped in a blanket of contentment and love.

- I am lovable.

- My parents love me.

- I am filled and nourished. I am content.

Guidelines for Healing with Meditations

In order for a visualization exercise to be truly effective, we must be able to not only imagine and inwardly see the scene, but to feel it emotionally as well. The more detail we add to the inner scene, the easier it is to feel it as real and the more effective it will be. Sights, sounds, smells, sensations, all help to make it a more complete and convincing experience. The subconscious accepts these as being real.

If we try to imagine a scene that is too far removed from our known experience, it will feel distant or unconnected to us, and thus it will not reach the emotional states needed to make it effective. One way of bridging the gap between the actual past and the imagined ideal is to go through a series of preliminary visualizations. We might start by remembering what actually happened, then mentally picturing it over again, changing it slightly with each repetition. Each consecutive time we imagine a new scene within, we can release some of the pent-up emotions from the old one and come closer to an ideal scene. Often, in fully experiencing their feelings, people begin to cry and go through other intense emotions. This is a real part of the healing process and should not be stopped or turned off. New information about what happened in childhood will probably arise and if properly handled this can be a very healing and integrating experience. The energy used to hold down these old feelings is then made available for constructive uses.

The visualization offered here represents an ideal experience of unconditional parental love. If we cannot imagine our parents hugging us as suggested, then we may visualize them at least talking to us in a positive manner. The next time, we can imagine them touching us almost affectionately, and then eventually embracing us.

If you cannot picture your own parents ever relating to you in this ideal manner, then choose or create in your mind parents or someone you respect that can. One method which has proven helpful is imagining some Spiritual figure, such as Jesus, or his mother Mary, or some person you look up to or love as your own Father or Mother. Many of us have now built a family of friends who give us what our own family was unable to give. If you cannot relate in any manner to the following suggested visualizations, then create your own. The important thing is that you experience what it is like to have an unmet need fulfilled and that you learn to know you are lovable and worthy to receive love. Then you can begin to love yourself.

Meditation for the First Year

Visualize yourself being picked up out of your crib and being held in your mother's and father's arms. Hear them telling you how long they have been yearning to have you and how much they love you. Bask in the warmth of their strong, comforting arms around you. As you see and feel their loving presence, notice how safe and nourished you are, how good it feels to be in their guiding and protecting presence. Imagine that Mom and Dad are doing the best they know how to fulfil your every need. Know that they are there for you. See them trying to deal with your frustrations with gentle, patient, loving attention. Feel the warmth of their caresses as you snuggle against them. Feel totally trusting and protected.

The Second Year

In the second year we begin to assert our *independent will.* We learn to reach out for the things we want and to say "No!" Our sense of ourself as a separate individual comes to us and we begin to act from inner feeling. Children who are prevented from developing this independence suffer from shame and self-doubt.

At this stage, we learn to explore and coordinate our bodies. Our successes in learning to talk and express ourselves, to walk and to run serve as a natural basis for self-confidence and autonomy. Although easily forgotten, these early triumphs are the blocks upon which we build our future successes in life.

Affirmations for the Second Year

- I am free to be me.

- I am special.

- I trust my feelings.

- I am free to express what I feel.

- I am fascinated by the miracle of life.

- I am a special part of creation.

- I am as playful as a kitten. I am as strong as a lion.

- I have already learned to walk and talk and I can do anything I choose.

Meditation for the Second Year

This particular visualization is not intended to create an ideal state. It is instead offered to aid in the enhancement of the will, if one felt this was a problem area. In the attainment of independent will, a child will go through a period in which it strives, by whatever means, to get what it wants. This could be termed blind will. If the parents cut off all the child's requests at this stage, then it tends to become very submissive to others and suffers from feelings of low self-esteem. If this is a issue for you, then try the following visualization.

Feel safe and relaxed. See yourself traveling back to your second year. Visualize yourself at a store or supermarket with your parents. You are fascinated by the various colors and shapes of the objects on the shelves. A large red package catches your attention. As you look closer you see an interesting-looking toy inside the box. You feel a strong urge to play with the toy. You tell your parents of your need but they gently tell you that you cannot have it. It seems strange to you that your parents are putting everything else into the cart except your toy.

Now see yourself in another part of the store reminding your parents of your desire. They respond more firmly: "No, you can not have it." You find this difficult to understand for you see the cart is being filled with lots of other things. You are sure that the toy will be fun to play with and will not harm anyone.

You now begin to holler for the toy in the red box. You notice that people are staring at you. Your parents emphatically tell you no, and that you must keep quiet. They do not respond to your request even when you begin to cry. You feel alienated and disappointed. Feel the tears running down your cheeks.

On the drive home you continually plead for the toy. At home you are relentless in your demand. Finally your parents tell you "Okay we will let you have it this time." They also try to explain why you cannot get everything you ask for. This seems very vague to you. All you know is that you are going to get your toy.

Now see one of your parents leaving the house and driving away. You wait patiently by the window, in silent anticipation. As he or she drives up and gets out of the car your heart leaps for joy as you see the bright red package in your parent's hand. You are overjoyed with excitement not only for the toy but because you were able to get your wish. Your parent now enters and gives you your toy and a hug. Satisfaction and contentment fills your being. You are happy that you were able to express your independent will and get your way.

Now be in the present moment sitting erect and tall knowing deep within that you are charged with unlimited power.

The Preschool Years

Play is the work of children and it is through play that *initiative* and creativity are developed. Our natural curiosity needs to be encouraged so that we may blossom in our own way. That is why God sent us to earth in the first place - to become unique and dynamic expressions of creation.

If our parents place undue importance on obedience and conformity, we never have the opportunity to become all we were created to be. We lose touch with our sense of inner direction and may spend our lives living out the wishes and expectations of others. This can produce a sense of anger and discontentment for a life not fully lived.

This is the time when our curiosity can introduce us to a world of wonder, and help us to develop our creativity. Through play, we learn to enjoy life with a sense of exuberance and fun.

Affirmations for the Preschool Years

- My job is to play and have fun.

- The world is my playground.

- There are wonders everywhere for me to discover and enjoy.

- My life is a land of magic.

- I am free to create anything I think of.

- I am full of life and happiness.

- Life is fun.

Meditation for the Preschool Years

If you want to re-establish or strengthen the qualities of initiative and creativity, try the following visualization.

Visualize yourself in your favorite play area. See all your prized toys spread out before you, inviting you to play with them. Picture yourself picking up one and having fun with it.

Now create a world of make believe where you can be as free and spontaneous as your heart desires. Express all your ideas and feelings in this creative world of fantasy. See yourself beaming with delight. Now carry the spirit of this world of limitless freedom and imagination into your everyday affairs.

The School Years

During this period we develop a sense of *achievement* through building things in the spirit of play. If we are placed in situations where we cannot successfully accomplish what is expected of us, we will tend to feel inferior and inadequate. We may go through life believing that we just cannot make the grade and that success is out of our reach. We are likely to become loners, feeling alienated from others.

Children need a good deal of encouragement and guidance during this phase of their lives. Parents and teachers can do much to stimulate children's desire to undertake and complete particular tasks. They need to be taught that mistakes are a necessary part of learning, and not a defeat or a defect of character. It is important that they be encouraged in the process of learning just as much from a mistake as they do from an accomplishment.

At this stage we learn how to cooperate with others. We may join clubs, play games, and learn how to share our toys and belongings. We study the fascinating world around us and begin to understand how things work. We learn to read and to extend ourselves beyond our immediate family in our search for fun, understanding and comradeship.

Affirmations for the School Years

- Learning is fun.

- I can do whatever I set my mind to do.

- It's OK to make mistakes. That is how I learn.

- I enjoy developing my talents and skills.

- I like people and they like me.

- I am singing and skipping down the road of life.

- Life is an adventure.

- I am spontaneous and free as a soaring eagle.

Meditation for the School Years

The following guided visualization is designed to help you connect with feelings of pride in accomplishment.

See yourself surrounded by your friends, parents, and teachers. You are at school about to receive an award for an honored project that you have completed. Feel the love and admiration of all these people focused on you. Now see yourself presenting your project.

This project was a true labor of love and cherished in your heart. You are so proud of your accomplishment! Drink in the congratulations of your parents, friends, and teachers, as they admire what you have done. You feel completely safe and accepted as you share all you went through to bring the work to completion. See yourself smiling and glowing inside. Feel your heart overflowing with satisfaction and joy.

The Teenage Years

Our task as teenagers is to establish a personal belief system and sense of *identity*. Natural impulses especially prompt us to assert our independence at this time, when we are biologically programmed to begin to grow away from our parents' control and prepare to leave the nest. If our parents resist this process, and see it as unruliness or disobedience, there may be power struggles leading to blame and hurt feelings. At a time when we are reaching new levels of physical and mental capacity, society restrains us and says "wait."

At this time we need to acquire the determination and independence to explore who we are and what we want. We finish most of our physical growth and develop the ability to reason. Unencumbered by practical experience, we are full of enthusiasm for our own ideas and desires. Society does not usually share our enthusiasm. This can be a trying time for both parents and teenagers.

Affirmations for the Teenage Years

- I have my parents unconditional love and support as I reach out and spread my wings.

- I am free to be me.

- I am free to explore and establish healthy relationships beyond my family.

- I am a unique and separate individual, and have a right to my own values and beliefs.

- I claim my own power to create the life that fulfills me.

- I will safely and joyfully pass through all transitions.

- I am a dynamic bud that is about to blossom into a full blooming flower.

Meditation for the Teenage Years

If, like most people, this stage has been difficult for you, you may wish to practice the following visualization.

See yourself in your room at home. Try to remember as much detail as you can about your room. See yourself sitting on the edge of your bed, or where you did most of your thinking and decision-making. Recall your major struggles. Now visualize someone you deeply trust and admire. It can be someone who is living today, in the past, or someone you have created in your imagination. This person is all-knowing, all-loving, and extremely sympathetic to your needs and desires. Imagine this perfect advisor walking across the room and coming to sit beside you. Mentally have a conversation in which the teenage you talks openly and honestly about your major concerns. Now listen to what your advisor says and feel how good it is to be totally understood, accepted, admired and given loving, helpful guidance.

Early Adulthood

In early adulthood we choose our goals and establish our commitments. It is a time to develop the quality of *intimacy* which requires loyalty and unselfishness. Instead of losing one's freedom, commitment - a prerequisite to true intimacy - leads to a state of expansion wherein we extend ourselves to feel for and do for others. We may take on the responsibilities of family life and learn to nurture others, making their welfare as important as our own.

Many people fear commitment, regarding it as a trap because in the past it has brought pain. This prevents one from following through in being at one's best for others or from having the determination to accomplish real goals. Instead of intimacy, many people experience isolation, and tend to escape into fantasy. Addictions to alcohol, drugs, sex, and other mood-altering activities may be used to compensate for or to dull the deep longing to connect with others, which is a basic human drive.

We can also give our loyalty and commitment to an ideal or to a humanitarian cause. We can be loyal to our dream, a group, a gang, our country, etc. Yet we need to be careful that we do not use this as a substitute for belonging in a family or some other fulfilling relationship. Fanaticism or bigotry often reflect this distortion of our primal need for intimacy and importance to others. The important thing is for us to choose our goals and focus our efforts toward their achievement with clarity and awareness, rather than putting them aside for what we think others expect of us.

Affirmations for Early Adulthood

- I find real freedom in commitment.

- I achieve excellence through inner work and discipline.

- I know I will achieve my dreams.

- By caring for myself, I help maintain society and the good of all.

- I enjoy being emotionally open with those I trust and love.

- I keep the compass of my mind focused on my goals.

- I say yes to life.

Meditation for Early Adulthood

These visualizations are designed to strengthen the qualities of commitment and loyalty to another individual or to your work or other goals.

Exercise 1

If you and a partner are going through any major difficulties or you feel the need to work on a relationship, here is a suggested visualization. Mentally see the image of your partner as vividly as you can. Reflect on all the good times you have spent together. Choose one memory that is special and visualize this many times until all the wonderful feelings come back to you. Now pick a difficult time in your relationship and reflect on the way that both of you resolved it. Bring yourself back to the present and see yourself listening intently to all that your partner has to say. You are not interrupting or formulating defensive arguments, explanations or thoughts of retaliation. See yourself simply listening and when the time is appropriate responding calmly and tactfully with your point of view. Feel that you have the flexibility to compromise when necessary. See yourself totally committed to this relationship and having the patience and resolve to make it work. See both of you reaching a point of compromise or agreement that does not negate either of you.

Exercise 2

Visualize your partner again. Try to feel that you two are blending becoming one in your intent to solve your problems. See yourself stepping into his or her body and mind. From this perspective try to feel what that person's needs and desires are. Travel through his or her memory files and do your best to understand the makeup of this person's belief system. Look out at the world through this person's eyes and appreciate his or her perceptions and opinions. Now step back into yourself. From these insights reflect on how you can have a deeper and more satisfying relationship with that individual. See how you can fulfil both your needs and bring peace and cooperation into your lives.

Exercise 3

See yourself committed to your work or goals. If you are having difficulty in this area, visualize a time when you were very successful in reaching one of your goals. If your record for successfully accomplishing your goals has been very low, then practice the following visualization as if through the eyes of someone who has accomplished something in his or her field of expertise.

Reflect back on the initial formulation of that goal and all the steps it took to bring the project to its successful completion. See how you or this person was able to rise above all obstacles. Charged with the enthusiasm of this accomplishment, plan how you will adapt these insights into your present situation. Visualize that you are now passionately committed to and successful in materializing your special dream.

The Middle Years

In the middle years we carry our goals forward and reap the rewards of our labor. The polarity in this stage is between *productivity* and self-absorption. We may be productive in our roles as parents, teachers, artists, businessmen and women, or in any other occupation that serves society. Naturally our dreams and goals may change throughout life. Whatever our outward expression, we require discipline and continued enthusiasm to manifest our loftiest goals.

If we become unclear about our initial resolve, we may abandon our commitment not only to our work but to our relationships as well. This is especially true if we feel we are not accomplishing our goals. We may sense that time is running out and make drastic changes in our attempts to feel worthy and that we are accomplishing something or being fulfilled. This phenomenon is commonly known as the mid-life crisis. Parts of ourselves that have not been integrated, or honored, talents or desires not pursued, can cause us difficulty. If we have not resolved our childhood issues, they tend to surface and become especially painful now. Any sudden, impulsive and drastic change usually ends in disappointment and regrets later on. Well-planned and carefully executed changes can lead to tremendous growth and power.

Affirmations for the Middle Years

- I will relax and allow all things in my life to unfold in their proper order.

- I keep myself physically, mentally, and spiritually fit.

- I find joy in creative work, using my reason, my will, and my activities to bring me fulfillment.

- I am a focal point of Universal energy, which flows through me in creative abundance.
  All my work is a unique contribution to mankind, according to God's plan.

- I realize I have accomplished a great deal.

- I am dancing to the tune of success.

Meditation for the Middle Years

Visualize yourself successfully accomplishing your life's dream. See that the results you have achieved are far beyond your dreams. Before you is a sea of smiling faces that have benefitted from your words and your work. Now notice that financial abundance and prosperity are also yours as the result of your efforts. Feel absolutely wonderful and proud of yourself for being able to not only materialize your dream but create such an all round success of your life as well. In your enthusiasm know that you are able to create even more successes.

Old Age

The quality that is inherent in this stage is the acquirement of *wisdom*. Life has been compared to an experiment in which we try to find, often through trial and error, the formula for successful living and contentment. Counsel and guidance has usually been sought out and accepted from members of society who have achieved wisdom. Many cultures down through the ages have valued and held their elders in the high esteem. Unfortunately our culture has been slanted toward youth and is only now beginning to value its older members and their accomplishments.

Many people still enjoy good health and vitality during old age. A healthy diet, exercise, and a positive attitude are important factors in maintaining vigor and longevity. Research has shown that the main factor is often a lively interest in and enthusiasm for life. This can come through the continuation of creative work, a hobby, or community service. Retired people often spend their time volunteering and making a personal contribution to their communities or to a worthy cause. Some share their life's experiences through writing or on tape for their family or for publication.

Older people are often good companions and caregivers for the young. They develop loving relationships with grandchildren and other young people which are of mutual benefit to everyone involved.

The most significant task of this stage is the care of the soul. Many turn to inspirational Spiritual writings as a way of finding meaning in their lives. Prayer and meditation may become a delight and all-satisfying as it leads to a closer communion with God. These comforting practices are also helpful in transferring the sense of identification from the mortal body to the immortal soul.

Affirmations for Old Age

- I give of my time, experience, and energy to better the world.

- I am proud of my hard-won wisdom, and can now use it to help those who can benefit from it.

- I can relax and enjoy the fruits of my labors.

- I can now do the things I really enjoy.

- I have woven the tapestry of my life with threads of love and all is well.

- I am now free to enjoy my best memories.

- I rejoice in the beauty of nature all around me.

- I now have the time to do the things I've always wanted to do.

- I have the time now to seek to know and commune with the One who created me.

● I am loved and respected in these, the best years of my life.

Meditation for Old Age

In this visualization imagine that you are an elder of a tribe. In this tribe the elders are held in the highest regard. Now see the peaceful essence of the evening all around you. You can smell the smoke of the campfires which have been started to take the chill off the autumn night. You see yourself walking through a forest. Reaching a clearing by a lake, you feel happy to be back at your favorite retreat area. This sacred ceremonial ground is where you have heard the wisdom of many inspiring elders.

Tonight is special, for you have been chosen by your fellow elders to share your wisdom. The sacred fire has already been lit. Everything is in readiness for your talk. People are arriving to hear your message. They are dressed in their finest clothes. Some of the other elders come and place sacred herbs on the fire and the aroma fills the night. There is electric energy in the air as the singers chant the Ancient Sacred Songs.

It now becomes clear to you how popular and respected you are. Never have you seen so many brothers and sisters come to the ceremonial grounds. As a result of the multitude that have arrived, the other elders decide to place you in a boat on the lake. Entering the boat you turn around and see the smiling faces of those who are eager to hear your message. The full moon bathes everything with its silvery light. There is the sound of water gently lapping on the side of the boat. In this atmosphere of peace you begin to tell of your experiences and the wisdom you have acquired over the years.

People are awed by your insightful message. At the completion of your talk there is a prolonged silence. Your wisdom has touched the minds and hearts of everyone. You can feel the love and respect of the tribe filling your being. The elders begin softly chanting once again and the entire tribe joins in. At the conclusion of the singing you lead everyone in a prayer of thanksgiving for the Creator's bounty. The tribe once again sits in silence drinking in your wisdom and the beauty of the night. People then slowly and quietly begin to leave and return to their homes. The other elders come to help you from the boat and they embrace you. You feel peaceful and complete. In silence you offer your Creator your heartfelt gratitude and love.

The End of Life

Depending on the past quality of an individual's life and his or her present attitude, we often see older people who are at one of two extremes - very bitter or extraordinarily calm and loving. At this stage of life we are therefore confronted with a choice between *inner peace* or despair. The need to make this decision can also come when we are seriously ill or thinking about our own mortality. The serious illness or death of a loved one may also bring this decision to mind.

At the end of life our consciousness goes more and more within and we may spend a great deal of time dwelling on memories and on thinking about life after death. At this stage greater importance needs to be placed on the discovery of the soul rather than on outward works and accomplishments. We realize we are going to have to gradually give up many external things such as our possessions, and in time even the body itself.

Those who achieve inner peace usually do so on the basis of Spiritual values and have learned identification with that part of themselves which is eternal. They are unafraid of death, because they see it as a natural transition and an opportunity for advancement. There awakens an awareness of a God who cares and is leading them to their highest and best good. The people who fall into this category find it easy to surrender to whatever comes and radiate a natural sweetness and contentment as they come to the end of their time on earth.

Affirmations for the End of Life

- I am not my Body. I am an immortal soul.

- I am eternal. My essence is unchanging.

- God is all love, all mercy.

- I can go forth in perfect peace knowing that my Creator is with me wherever I go.

- I accept my life as I have lived it, and now move with courage and hope toward the transition to come.

- God, as infinite love and beauty, is leading me to a wondrous place that is exactly right for me.

- Love will carry me to my eternal abode.

- I am a glorious butterfly soon to emerge from the cocoon that has held me.

Meditation for the End of Life

Visualize yourself at the end of life. See yourself sitting in your favorite chair. You are peacefully aware that death is near. There is no fear, only joyous expectation. You are grateful to have this insight and the opportunity to peacefully prepare for your final transition.

Now imagine yourself making contact with your loved ones. You enjoy and cherish their love, friendship, and loyalty. See yourself trying to work out any unresolved conflicts that may still exist. Travel down the highway of your memory and enjoy all the achievements you have accomplished, what you are proud of. Forgive yourself for the things you felt that you could have handled more effectively, or about which you have regrets.

A change in consciousness gently overcomes you. You can feel your energies and attention being drawn within. A flash of your entire life passes before you. Your breath stops but you feel no pain only a feeling of lightness and expansion. Your body of light is beginning to float out of your physical form. A Spiritual Being materializes before you and helps you out of your physical body. Trustingly you look at this Being who is shimmering in light. Looking at yourself you see you are also scintillating with the same light. As you float upwards you can see your lifeless body in the chair below you. You feel peaceful and free of all earthly concerns.

Now visualize yourself and your Spiritual Guide floating through a multicolored tunnel. At the other end you recognize loved ones who have already passed on welcoming you. They are young and beautiful. What touches you most of all is how radiant and happy they are, and how good it is to be with them again.

A glorious white light now appears in front of you. This light is more radiant than a million suns yet very gentle and mild. A resonate and compassionate voice resounds out of the light. You know deep within your soul that this is a manifestation of Divine Love that has appeared for you. The loving voice asks you "How much did you love and what did you learn?" You pour out your heart in complete honesty and trust to this Supreme Loving Presence. You are not judged nor are faults dwelt upon. You are encouraged to be the best you can be and reclaim your status as a son/daughter of God. The white light slowly disappears leaving you in an aura of loving understanding. The Spiritual Being comes over and embraces you. You know you will now move into a new and wonderful life.

Inner Healing

By practicing the suggested affirmations and meditations for the different stages of life, we can consciously reclaim and strengthen our self-esteem. We may find, however, that certain areas still need extra work. If you want to work on these issues more deeply, the following exercises are suggested to help cleanse your mind and heart.

Healing Affirmations

- With the strength of God within me, I face whatever challenges today will bring.

- I invite my inner feelings to come out into the light of my conscious acceptance.

- I respect all parts of my being, and now allow them to freely intermingle and come into a new alignment for my highest good.

- My limiting patterns are melting in the sun of God's love.

- I am open to the potential for change to bring me a full and beautiful life.

- I take responsibility for my present circumstances, and know that whatever I have created I also have the power to change to something much better.

- I am in charge of my life. I am breaking free of all limitations from the past and taking for myself the power to create my future.

- I am determined to overcome all obstacles so that I may experience the best life has to offer.

Healing Meditation

Find a comfortable position. Be sure your spine is straight and your mind is alert. Be still and close your eyes. Visualize yourself surrounded with God's love in the form of beautiful, soft light. Feel the light falling on your face and body, relaxing and soothing you. Feel the light penetrating more deeply and saturating every cell of your body. All tensions are melting away.

Now visualize your heart. See your heart muscle pumping blood throughout your body providing nourishment for the cells. Looking more closely at your heart you can see a delicate pink light surrounding and penetrating it. Watch this heart of light softly glowing and circulating feelings throughout your body and mind. Notice that the brilliance of the pink light is tarnished by some small, muddy dark patches. These dark areas represent feelings of frustration, grief, resentment and other life-diminishing emotions. As you watch you can see these dark spots preventing the harmonious flow of the pink light of love and self-confidence.

Now visualize a small door in your chest near the heart. You control this passage and can open it as much as you want to. Open this door as far as you feel comfortable and ready to receive God's healing light. Watch the light gently flowing through the door and beginning to dissolve the muddy areas and restore the pink light to its natural brilliancy. Let this process take place at it's own pace until you are a clear channel of the light of Universal Love.

Now visualize your brain with its grayish matter containing countless crests and valleys. As you explore your brain you can see innumerable electrical impulses being emitted by the neurons. Your brain is aglow with dynamic energy feeding the billions of brain cells. Imagine vibrant dancing balls of colored lights floating in the valleys of your brain. These thought forms appear as different shades of colors according to their degree and quality.

Calm thoughts are beautiful delicate shades of blue. Thoughts of unconditional love vibrate as soft warm pink. Joyous thoughts dance in the hue of sunshine yellow. Orange balls of light denote confidence and courage. Strength and power wear the armor of vibrant red. You are probably going to notice that there are some dark grey or black balls floating throughout your brain. These dark spheres are slow and sluggish, representing thoughts of inferiority, worry and other limitations. They often collide with the bright colored balls preventing the positive thoughts from flowing effectively through your mind and on to your heart.

Now create a door on the top of your heard. This door can also be opened as much as you like according to your comfort level. As you open the door see God's perfect light flowing in and flooding your brain. Watch as the light engulfs the dark balls and transforms them into colored ones of a positive nature. Your brain begins to glow more and more brightly as it radiates the Divine Light. Now feel a wonderful change in your consciousness. See how much better and more optimistic you feel. You are now aware that you can accomplish everything fine and good that you desire. See your heart and brain working harmoniously together to bring you a full and balanced life.

Changing Limiting Beliefs

Choose one of your inner beliefs that you would like to change. Spend time thinking back to how and when you acquired it, and what you would like to believe instead. Write down the specific old belief that you want to leave behind and also the new empowering one. For example, if you sometime acquired the belief "I don't have much musical talent", and this has prevented you from doing something you would like to do with music, you might want to substitute the belief "I <u>do</u> have musical talent" and go ahead and develop it.

While you are practicing the following exercise, mental images or phrases from the past may spontaneously come up. For example, you may see your parents' faces and hear them telling you, "It's a waste of time for you to buy a guitar. You'll never play it." Record whatever comes up to interfere with your new belief, and find ways to creatively handle it. Realize that it was not necessarily true at all and that you may have quite a bit of talent.

Book of Beliefs Meditation

Feel peaceful and relaxed. Close your eyes and enter deep within yourself. Now visualize yourself traveling to another sphere of consciousness. In this plane of existence everything is vibrant and refined. You are free to travel to any planet that you wish. You find yourself landing on a warm and friendly planet that looks very similar to earth. A spiritual being meets you who is anciently familiar. You feel comfortable and at peace with this Presence. Your guide leads you on a tour of this beautiful planet. On your travels you are directed into a large white marbled building which contains countless chambers. On one of these you see your name inscribed on the doorway. Your guide takes out a key and opens the door for you. Upon entering you see different objects that remind you of your past. On the shelves are various books and scrolls. Your guide takes down a book entitled "My Beliefs" and hands it to you.

Opening the book you see that it contains a record of your belief system. As you study the book your Guide helps you to recognize certain beliefs that you know are not beneficial for you. You realize the time has come to do something constructive about them. See yourself removing the page from the book that records one belief you most want to change. You tear this page into many pieces to implant in your mind that this belief is no longer valid. You notice a fireplace in the corner of the room which is crackling with a glowing fire. Walking over to the fireplace you throw the pieces of paper into the fire. Feel an inner satisfaction as you watch that belief disappearing in the flames.

Your guide motions you over to a desk that contains various writing materials. You intuitively understand that you are to create a new page and register a positive and enriching belief which will be an asset in your life. You spend a great deal of time thinking of this new belief. You know that "My Beliefs" is a book of your history and what you place on this new page and put in the book will become a part of your life. You are therefore very careful to record exactly what you want to happen in your life. You then put the page back into the book and hand the book to your Guide. He smiles with approval and places the book back on the shelf.

Your guide now asks you to sit down and close your eyes. You are assured that you can return to this beautiful and serene planet any time you choose. As you close your eyes you feel your consciousness leaving this plane of existence and traveling back to your earthly home. Opening your eyes you look around at the familiar setting but you know that something has changed profoundly. You are intensely aware that your belief system has changed and you are now making plans to make this new belief a tangible reality in your everyday life.

LOVING OTHERS

The Universal Plan

Love is unity and harmony. By Its power, *Universal Love draws us together until we are reunited in Spirit.* Through Love, the various forces of the universe come into being. Universal Love harmonizes the forces of attraction and repulsion to maintain what is called the cosmic dance.

The power of Love pulls at the hearts of men and women, that they may unite their lives in an expression of love, one for the other. Ideally our love expands as we learn to love and care for our families.

We learn to expand our consciousness and develop the Spiritual qualities of compassion and unselfishness through caring about others. Infinite Love yearns to unfold and bring everything into oneness. Through Its workings men and women begin to expand their love to include their neighbors, then their community, nation, and the world. The magic of Love extends to include all created things.

Ideally, under the influence of Love, everyone will eventually feel unconditional love for all. We will no longer be limited by our own personal wants and desires, but will be concerned with the welfare of all people and of the whole world. Our sense of identity will then expand to include all creation and we will realize that all things are united in Universal Love. We will know then that what we do unto others we also do unto ourselves, and that God's will - what is for the best good of all - is also what is for our own best good.

Real Love

Perfecting various human relationships is an important part of the Spiritual path, but still will not bring complete satisfaction. Our contacts and dealings with one another help us become whole and to aid each others' development. Love is active only when we consciously choose to do what expands ourselves <u>and</u> others in Spiritual growth. This attitude requires both self-understanding and a dynamic act of will.

True love tunes into the wisdom of the cosmos and acts accordingly. Godlike love is not a pleasurable feeling of the body that is termed "making love," nor is it the act of falling in love, nor the romantic love a person feels when attracted to and infatuated with another human. *Real love is a total commitment to the highest spiritual unfoldment of ourselves and others.*

The world tends to glorify romantic love, and insists that this state is the supreme goal of love and life itself. If a person does not have it or is not in the process of seeking it, then in the eyes of the world that person is sorely deprived. The myth is that to be healthy and truly happy, a person needs to find a perfect mate and become so intertwined that they move and live as one person until the end of time. The delusion continues further with the belief that if partners do not continually feel this romantic love, something is wrong with the relationship, and they must not be destined for each other.

Love is not an exclusive dependency, but rather an expansion to include others and the world. In ordinary romantic love two people try to lose themselves in each other. This merging, in which both partners tend to act as one, is mistakenly thought of as true intimacy. In this state of fusion, loneliness tends to disappear for a time, but the phenomenon is only temporary. It is dependency in the name of love and can also occur in other forms of relationship such as between friends, and between parents and children.

Physical and mental attraction may have been the spark that brought a couple together in the first place. When the biological and emotional feelings subside, each person tends to drop the facade which they at first displayed in order to impress the other and to keep the romance alive. The couple is then confronted head-on with their differences. If at this point the two so involved decide to truly commit to growing and helping each other grow, accepting and cherishing their differences, then they will have tuned into the higher purpose of Love, and real love will have begun.

Mature Love - Acceptance of Differences

When two people who are not strong in their own sense of self "fall in love," they are unconsciously looking for someone to take care of them and make them feel good about themselves. Such relationships are not grounded in the ideal of wanting each partner to grow into his or her potential, but are attempts to fill holes in individual personalities. They are actually trying to get something from the other, using the partner as an object to satisfy their own needs. This is the opposite of being concerned with giving love from a sense of overflowing completeness.

Although most of us are unaware of it, very often we are seeking the things we did not get in our relationship with our parents. We may be attracted to those qualities in a partner that we feel we are lacking. When we mature emotionally and Spiritually, we are firmly rooted in our own uniqueness or "I"-ness. We do not get wrapped up in others to the point where we lose our identity. Instead, we operate from our own solid sense of who we are, and know that no other person can fulfil us. We recognize that we ourselves are responsible for our own happiness and completeness, and don't expect a partner to do it for us.

Individuals who enter into an unhealthy relationship find their boundaries collapse and this results in enmeshment or false intimacy. This leads to problems such as co-dependency, power struggles, etc. But when two mature individuals commit to loving each other unconditionally and are willing to sacrifice for one another, they begin to *expand* their boundaries. Mature individuals expand their boundaries to include their partner. From this state of awareness they can then accept and enjoy differences without feeling threatened by them. This makes for a much more comfortable sharing and gives fertile ground for individual growth.

Aspects of Love Relationships

Pure Divine love flows into human hearts through the filters of many different types of relationships: parental and conjugal love, friendships and the relationship between a Spiritual master and disciple. If we can perfect any one of these aspects, then we begin to approach Divine Love.

Parental Love

Women are usually more feeling-oriented, and men tend to function more through reason. A mother usually feels a strong sense of love for her child. As soon as her baby is born, she instinctually wants to hold the child and draw it close. Her feelings are attuned to the child, and she can usually sense when it is in distress or in need. This bonding of a mother with her child can last for an entire lifetime.

Ideally, a mother's love is unconditional. No matter what mistakes her child makes, she tends to be ever-ready to forgive. Even if a child goes down the wrong avenues of life and commits serious offenses, a real mother's love is still there with understanding, comfort, and support.

A father ideally wants to protect his child. He realizes that he needs to take care of the family, and works to provide food, shelter, and financial security. Through wisdom a father understands that he has a responsibility to instruct and guide the child along the path of life. If a child asks for something, a father tends to analyze the situation before giving an answer, whereas a mother will more likely try to satisfy the child's need with whatever feels right at the time.

Both fathers and mothers work in accord with Universal Love when they give unselfishly of themselves, helping their children grow to their maximum potential. By giving children quality time, parents instill a sense of value. This is crucial to their development.

Like falling in love, the love of a father and mother for their child is to some degree instinctual. Along with the mating instinct, nature also induces this feeling of love for a child in order to propagate the species. Parents, being human, may make mistakes along the way, but they generally try to raise their children according to what they believe is right.

Conjugal Love

The Creator embodies both Feeling and Reason. *One of our main lessons in life is to learn to balance the feeling side of our nature with the reasoning side.* Men and women are created equal, even though generally speaking men are physically stronger. Women tend to operate more from feeling, men more from reason. Ideally, marriage helps men and women to attain a balance of these qualities and to attune their natures with Spirit. It is also possible to balance these qualities inwardly, without the need of a partner.

Unfortunately, in our society many couples do not understand this principle. They unite, attracted to the qualities in their partner that they admire, but feel are lacking in themselves. After a while, however, the woman may begin to feel that her husband does not seem to care about her feelings. At times he may appear to be too much in his head - unfeeling and uncompassionate. When she is having a problem and looking for understanding and wants her feelings supported, he may instead try to offer her hard facts about why she should not feel this way, and why she ought to snap out of it. When she feels something very strongly, the husband may laugh it off as being illogical and absurd. This is devastating to a person who feels deeply.

Similarly, the husband may have worked out something very concrete in his mind regarding a project. He may have looked at every angle, thought it out carefully, and come up with what he thinks is the most logical choice. Upon telling his wife, and expecting credit for his insight, she may instead dismiss his point of view because to her it does not feel right. No matter what facts and figures he may offer, she does not budge because she is rooted in her feelings.

Communication breaks down as each partner begins to feel that the mate does not understand them. A man retreats into his thoughts and a woman into her feelings, and this usually creates a real barrier between them. Both often respond to situations based on semiconscious thoughts, feelings, and beliefs. If these can be openly discussed, it is much easier to achieve understanding.

Women and men need to be respectful of each others' feelings and opinions. It is in honest sharing that the union of feeling and reason can occur. Union does not happen just because two people have been joined together by a ceremony recognized by law. The balance of heart and head needs to be worked on constantly throughout the marriage.

Both men and women have a need to perfect their own natures. A man can grow and mature as he learns to own and express his feelings and to share them. When reason is developed, and balanced with feeling it can become the all-knowing quality of intuition. When an individual works from intuition, he or she is in tune with Universal Wisdom. If a man's reason is based only on thinking and logic, then his sense of reality will probably be altered by prejudice and bias.

A woman needs to claim the masculine side of her being. She needs to strive to balance her feelings with logic and reason. Ordinarily, feelings are colored by individual preferences and emotions. When feeling is intelligently developed, it can mature into intuition and Oneness with Universal Love.

Marriage is an opportunity to unite with another person in body, mind and soul - to care for and support another <u>as one cares for and supports one's self</u>. Unselfish service to others is a divine quality but not if it is done at the expense of self.

Unity with another through Unconditional Love, understanding and friendship can brings a soul into union with Universal Love, but it cannot be done by sacrificing self and its needs.

The Love of Friends

In loving one's friends there is the element of free choice. This is also true for a man and woman before marriage. After the marital ceremony, however, husband and wife are supposed to love one another unconditionally.

If marriage is not based on friendship, then this legal binding may bring in the element of compulsion. People may expect or demand love from partners simply because they are married; they tend to feel they have a right to the other's love, and that their partner should strive to make them happy regardless of their own behavior. Ideally, husband and wife should also be each other's best friend.

When loving friends, one is not influenced by a drive to mate or dominate. Love is usually given as a free gift, not just because it is expected. In this sense, friendly love is very pure. It is possible for it to exist in all relationships, between man and woman, woman and woman, and man and man. It tends to be hardest to keep in the close confines of marital relationships.

In human friendship we can learn the art of giving ourselves freely and openly. After this giving of ourselves spontaneously to friends, we can then come to the point where we want to commit ourselves totally to Universal Love. Then we will explore Divine friendship with all human beings. All who cross our path, even if it were what was once an enemy, can become the object of our Divine friendship.

Spiritual Love

Spiritual love is the grandest of human loves because it is the reconnection with the love of God. Spiritual masters see God in all beings and unconditionally work for the upliftment of humankind. For example, Jesus was in tune with Love's highest purpose and worked for His disciples' spiritual unfoldment. The disciples loved and trusted Jesus because they realized that He was leading them to the Love of God. Spiritual masters who are already united with Universal Love are complete within themselves. They have nothing to gain but the joy of bringing others to Divine Love. The love they receive from their disciples is given directly to the heart of God.

Loving and Getting Along with Others

Vibrational Attraction to Family and Associates

Divine Intelligence, in cooperation with each of our own higher selves, has placed us in our present family and general life situation. *The environment and people drawn to us are in accord with what we need for our own individual growth.* Our present circumstances represent what we need for our growth and development. The challenges we face are designed to help us overcome our limitations and show us the constructive actions we need to take.

When we understand how our choices and our actions have been responsible for our being where we are, we will no longer blame anyone else for our fate. Individuals having marital problems who believe things would be better if they were married to someone else, will usually be disillusioned when they make a change. If a person gets a divorce and does not inwardly and outwardly work on the problems that plagued them in their marriage, then the same problems and situations will arise again. The outer form may be different but the inherent problems will be the same, because the inner person has not changed. We take ourselves with us wherever we go.

Similarly, in a work situation we may feel that if only a certain individual were removed, things would be great. If that other individual leaves, but the particular lesson or issue is not resolved, then sooner or later someone else will come into our life to present the same lesson. This will keep happening until we look at what it is in ourself that makes us react to a certain type of person or situation in the way we do.

The Universe is exact and just in its dealings, and everything is right on schedule. As soon as we realize that we unconsciously attract situations that test us, we are then free to use these as opportunities for learning. Once we change ourselves, a similar situation will no longer be a problem for us.

Truly Loving Others

Consideration for others is considered admirable by all religions and by society in general. Saintly souls give spontaneously from the heart, without thought of return. In the Christian world, many Saints, such as Mother Teresa of Calcutta, perceive Christ in their suffering brothers and sisters. In serving Him "in His distressing disguises," these great souls know that they are truly serving God.

Service to others moves out of the realm of love when it is performed with a sense of duty, coercion, or sacrifice. For example, a woman who stays in an abusive situation may be rendering service not from love, but from fear. She may go to extraordinary lengths to please her husband because she is afraid of incurring his anger, or because she is afraid of losing his financial support. It is important that we be honest with ourselves and know our true motives, so that we can do whatever is necessary to nurture ourselves and maintain our self-esteem. True service is never rendered at the expense of

ourselves. That kind of service causes unconscious resentment
which harms us and does not fulfil its purpose.

Honest Expression of Feeling

Fear and anger are human emotions and have their place
and value. Some people tend to label these feelings
unspiritual, and pretend to be loving when inwardly they are
boiling with anger. We all need to learn to deal with our
underlying feelings in a constructive way. To suppress anger
and pretend to be above it does not work in the long-term. It
will come out in other, often quite unpleasant, ways.

It is important for us to realize that the ability to be
courageously assertive is appropriate in most situations.
Righteous anger, if it truly is about something that is wronging
us, gives us the strength to initiate change and to stand up for
our rights under difficult conditions. This prevents us from
becoming victims of other people's inappropriate behavior.
Even Jesus demonstrated this in throwing the money changers
out of the Temple.

Fear can also be useful and appropriate. It stimulates us to
be cautious in the face of danger. A moderate amount of
anxiety can help us stay alert. Intense fear, however, is
paralyzing, and prevents us from functioning well.

Although fear and anger are not of the essence of the soul,
honest expression helps us to resolve conflicts. It also leads to
our higher growth, because the suppression of emotions can
actually block the path to God. Suppressed emotions will
sooner or later come out with carping or complaining, or with
violent reactions to small triggers, or even in bodily illness.

The Art of Balance

Balance is golden; it is harmony with the universe and with ourselves.   Buddha taught the golden Middle Path to his followers and counseled them to avoid extremes.   The first pitfall to avoid was "overindulgence" in sensual pleasures, or unnatural and useless preoccupations with things of the world. The second pitfall was "over-renunciation," which can result in unholy practices of self-torture and ill-health.   Buddha claimed that he achieved enlightenment by following the Middle Path of balance.

It is important to realize that to go to any extreme can turn a virtue into a vice.   When this occurs, the positive quality is no longer a benefit but becomes a detriment.   Such lack of balance within ourselves is usually the cause of our difficulties with others.

If we claim to practice humility, and under this guise allow others to abuse us or our family, then what we are calling humility turns into cowardliness.   If we militantly stand up for ourselves and hurt people in the process, then this firmness turns into insensitivity.   In interacting with others, balance is the key factor.

Thoughts on Balance

● In dealing with others we need to be sure we are neither too frivolous nor too serious.

● There is an art of knowing when it is time to laugh and have fun and when it is time to work.

● Meeting others half-way often leads to mutual understanding and growth.

● Perfectionist tendencies, although sometimes appropriate, tend to create stress in one's life, and often do not result in positive gain. There really are some things that do not need to be done perfectly.

- We need to learn to listen to the body's intelligence and to understand its needs and rhythms. For example, it is wise to know when and how much to feed it, and when to fast or refrain from feeding it.

- We need to learn flexibility. Rigidity can make life difficult for ourselves and those we associate with. Some people seem to fall apart if they do not have their morning coffee. This may also apply to health fanatics who are utterly dismayed if they miss their health drink in the afternoon. Any extreme shows we are out of balance.

Kindness Versus Moral Backbone

The Vedic scriptures, which are the oldest in the world, describe a man of God as "Softer than the flower, where kindness is concerned; stronger than the thunder, where principles are at stake." I have watched a documentary on the work of Mother Teresa of Calcutta which showed her carrying on her duties. I was deeply impressed with how she manifested this Vedic tradition. With the homeless and suffering she was pure compassion. There was such loving tenderness in her eyes. Yet, when she was dealing with businessmen regarding some building project, she was unshakable and firm. The look on her face was then one of iron will, and it was quite obvious to all that she was in charge and unwavering in her resolve.

As children of the Infinite, we need to develop both sides of our nature. In some situations we need to surrender to the flow, and in others we need to stand up for ourselves or for what we believe in. Often, we feel awkward when we waver between the qualities of gentleness and strength. Unfortunately, it is not always easy to know which is appropriate.

Many of us have developed one side of our nature more than the other. We may continue to be sweet of speech, when we really need to be firm and draw the line on some inappropriate behavior or abuse coming our way. In other words, we may have to develop and initiate moral strength. On the other hand, we may find that softness and compromise are contrary to our nature, and that may well be what we need to develop.

There is no exact formula for getting along with others. Each specific situation requires a balance of the heart and head. We need to call on both our reason and our feelings. The appropriate response will ultimately be the one that helps all individuals involved to grow from the situation.

Thoughts on Kindness

- People appreciate acts of kindness. Such acts help them to feel special, and increase their self-esteem.

- Offering words of encouragement wherever you see an opportunity is an act of love.

- To be courteous, considerate, and respectful of others and their opinions smooths the path of relationship. Others have a right to their opinions as much as we have to ours. The fact that someone differs with you does not mean they are against you. This misperception has ruined so many otherwise constructive exchanges.

- Patience and tolerance are tools that work well. Often we can see our own blind spots by really listening to others without taking differences as criticisms.

- When someone seeks, truly needs, and asks for your help, that is the time to give freely of your time and energy in whatever way will truly help and promote another's growth.

- To force your opinion, help or advice on anyone who has not asked for it violates that person's rights and usually does more harm than good.

- Concentrate on the best in others, instead of their faults. It brings out the best in both of you.

- When someone asks your advice, offer loving suggestions only, never judgments or condemnations. Never consider it an affront if someone does not follow what you suggest. We can never know all the circumstances that are impinging on someone else.

- Learn to be less concerned about how others treat you, and more concerned with how you treat others. This will pay untold dividends.

- If you feel someone has mistreated you, sending love and positive energy in return is the most effective thing you can do. It is surprising how this can change a situation.

- If others are physically or verbally abusive, know it is time to draw the line. You can withdraw to protect yourself, and initiate loving counter-alternatives when it is clear that you will not take abusive behavior.

- Quarrels and anger can be stilled by calmness and not getting your feelings involved. "He that is slow to anger is better than the mighty; and he that ruleth his spirit, better than he that taketh a city" Proverbs 16:32. Ancient but timely wisdom.

- Learn how to be silent, especially if you know that further conversation will lead to an argument. However, it is not wise to use silence as a means of wounding others. This stops all movement toward understanding and reconciliation.

- If someone confesses something they have done and are sorry, be ever ready to forgive and to withhold judgement.

- Watch what you say and notice if there is malice in it; if so, work to change it. Spend time thinking of better ways to phrase your conversation so there is no hurt or judgement in it.

Thoughts on Moral Strength

- When we are secure in our own worth, we can be fearless and unafraid without being judgmental. We need only to set limits on what we are willing to do, or to endure from others and kindly, but firmly, stick with our stand.

- When those around you are being negative and critical, gently let them know that their behavior is not acceptable. By being positive and upbeat you can turn the conversation or situation around.

- Learn to say "no" with authority when you are being used by others. This can be done kindly but firmly. One way is to say "That will not work for me." Explanations and argument are not necessary, and it is better to be firm and not get into them.

- Do not do for others what you know they can do for themselves. This does not serve the other person. It only props them up and takes away their initiative.

- Be sympathetic to others' problems, but not to the point that it disturbs your own peace of mind. You cannot help those who have fallen into a morass by jumping in with them.

- While helping others, it is effective to see them as inwardly perfect and healed. Constant sympathizing with problems will amplify distress and make the situation worse. Listen, but it is not helpful to wallow with them. Show confidence that they can find a way out. Get them to talk about other options.

Intimacy Versus Solitude

Intimacy is sharing life and experiences in an open exchange of ideas and feelings with another. Each person becomes sensitive to the thoughts and feelings of the other. Through this attunement each begins to do things spontaneously for the other without being asked. For example, a friend feels thirsty and the other friend will feel this intuitively and get him or her a glass of water.

When two people are in tune, there is a free flow of communication. There is trust. Each cares about the other's well-being and helps the other. In this manner, they are drawn closer to oneness with Universal Love.

The blending of intimacy and respectful distance between two people is crucial in any relationship. For inner balance, each of us needs to take some time and have some place to be alone in order to become secure in the Self. We may need time alone to meditate and pray so as to strengthen our personal connection with Spirit. We also need sufficient time to ourselves to review and plan our lives, and to accomplish personal projects.

The balance between solitude and intimacy is very important. At different times for each of us there is a need for more of one than the other. If this balance is lacking, it tends to lead to disharmony. When one partner wants more closeness than the other and feels needy and desperate for affection and recognition, this will eventually cause a division. The needy one will unconsciously try to manipulate and control the other to bring about the fulfillment of his or her own needs. Through these actions one tends to suffocate the other with a clinging need for love.

The reaction of the other will generally be to resent this invasion and to push the other away physically, mentally or emotionally. Experiencing this, the needy one has set him or herself up to feel rejected, which in turn increases the desperation to get love from the other. This cycle tends to escalate until the relationship deteriorates, often beyond recall.

Some people may naturally be detached, and need to spend a lot of time in solitude. These individuals sometimes feel they are being virtuous by being non-attached to the ways of the world. When a person avoids all intimacy with others, however, this can stem from a subconscious fear of being hurt or rejected.

Thoughts on Intimacy

- Intimacy is the art of sharing our special attributes and personal feelings with others. We open ourselves and are vulnerable and that promotes trust and respect between responsible individuals.

- We need to believe in ourselves, and trust that our partner is interested in what we have to say, so that we can have the confidence to communicate effectively.

- We need to let others know that we believe in them, and are interested in what they have to say honoring its importance to them. Careful listening is an art to be cultivated if intimacy is to flourish.

- People are entitled to feel and respond emotionally to any situation in their own way. We need to give them that freedom and claim it for ourselves.

- When in the presence of others, give them your undivided attention. Notice that when you feel the need to dominate the conversation you are really looking for confirmation for yourself.

- It works well to be sincerely interested in others' happiness by being aware of what they think they need, not what we think they should need.

- Prayer for the success and well-being of others, physically, mentally, and spiritually helps us tune into what others need and assists all concerned.

- Communication is the basis for understanding and harmony. If there is a disagreement, discuss the differences and listen for the other person's point of view without blame or judgement. This leads to reconciliation and mutual respect and closeness.

- Jealousy and suspicion come out of insecurity. By feeling confident of your own self-worth, you can deal with these negative and hurtful thought patterns and they will fade from your life.

- We need to really examine our expectations of others. If you accept people as they are, and don't expect something they may not be able to give, they can never disappoint you.

- It is wise never to take others for granted. Those around us all have something to teach us, and they, too, have their uncertainties and need attention and reassurance.

Thoughts on Solitude (Respectful Distance)

- Others have a right to their own privacy. Prying into someone's affairs does not promote intimacy. Just because two people are friends or are married does not give them the right to know everything about the other. Confidences are given freely when there is trust and respect.

- When you are coming into closeness with others, it is not necessary or useful to reveal or confess your every thought and feeling, especially if negativity is involved.

- If others are doing something that is important to them or are in deep concentration, it is the mark of respect not to disturb them unless it is absolutely necessary.

- We never have the right to treat others as if we own them. In our society males have tended to feel they own their wives, and parents feel that they own their children. No one owns anyone else. We are all individuals with our own rights.

- We need to exercise caution about making anyone feel trapped in a relationship, be it marriage, business, or any other. Those in prison do not love their jailors, and are sure to want to escape from them.

- To impose your will or desires on others, especially when it has been pointed out that it is not appreciated, engenders resentment rather than intimacy.

Changing Oneself

To help others learn and grow, the only effective course we can adopt is to change ourselves.. Each of us is the only person over whom we truly have control. If we want to help someone to be positive, our own positive vibration and actions are more effective than any sermon or remark.

We respect the admirable actions of others and feel inspired to be like them. On the other hand, we all tend to ignore or resent others who expose our faults and tell us what we ought to do. Sometimes we may even go so far as to purposely do the opposite.

It is much easier to recognize and point out others' faults than it is to look at our own. Our own faults are buried under years of rationalization and denial, and we have generally learned to excuse them. Sometimes the emotions that are associated with destructive thought patterns are very painful, and we find every reason not to look at them or to work on them. If we do come to see some of our maladaptive tendencies, it is common to get depressed about them and try to avoid the issue. This serves no one, especially ourselves.

If we pay close attention to the ways others react to us, we can learn much about ourselves. As hard as it is to do, we would gain much if we could welcome the feedback we receive from others, and honestly accept it without being resentful or hurt. To be thankful for constructive criticism shows real maturity and will speed our growth and take us out of the pain of repression and denial.

Thoughts on Changing Oneself

● In striving to better ourselves on all levels, we need to watch that we never try to gain something at the expense of others. If we are working to gain financial prosperity, it is important to remember that there is an abundance in the universe, and it will never serve us to gain money through another's loss. Sooner or later this will boomerang.

● Using critical or sarcastic words to a wrongdoer will only make that person defensive, and lead to the continuance of the behavior out of anger, rebellion, or even despair.

- If we see that we have done an injustice or hurt someone unnecessarily, then we need to immediately apologize with sincerity and dignity and make restitution where it is appropriate.

- If some innocent remark or action we have made triggers an overreaction in another, then we can work it out by asking to dialogue with the person, owning that we may have been careless, and thus giving that person the feeling that we care about him or her and providing an opportunity for the person to look at his or her own reaction patterns.

- Thinking of ourselves as victims, feeling hurt, or resentful when someone points out a fault or shortcoming will never contribute to our growth nor to our ability to have healthy and supportive relationships.

- If another person close to us does not ask for but truly needs our counsel, with much thought and care we may enter into a supportive conversation and encourage that person to see his or her own solution.

Honesty and Directness

People respect honesty. Those who always speak the truth, who are up front and direct, gain much in life and are recognized for their integrity. However tact and consideration are part of honesty and integrity.

It is important to remember that speaking the truth is only beneficial when it is appropriate and helpful. If someone goes around telling everyone that their friend John is an alcoholic and cannot hold his tongue while under the influence, then that statement, which may be true, is destructive. It is likely to cause John to become depressed when he hears what others have been told about his problem. It could well lead him to increase his drinking to drown his depression.   It also shows a lack of compassion on the part of the person spreading these truthful but hurtful insights.

Thoughts on Honesty

- Honesty still is the best policy when balanced with consideration and the desire to be helpful.   It is not necessary to blurt out everything we know.   We need to be true to ourselves and to consider the effect of what we say on others.

- Dependability will gain you friends and respect.

- If we want something from someone, the most effective way to get it is to be direct.   To skirt an issue, and then use manipulation or guilt to get what we want from another, will cause resentment and pain, and will work against us and not for us.

- To pretend to know more than we actually know is a form of dishonesty and will eventually boomerang.   On the other hand, we are under no obligation to advertise our lack of knowledge.   Sometimes it pays to remain silent.

- When we pretend to have a virtue to impress others, we are heading for a fall.

- If you know you lack a positive characteristic, then deliberately practice it.   This is not dishonesty, but an affirmation of your inner intention to gain that characteristic.

Getting Along with Others

- If we see ourselves and everyone else as children of God, it will be easier to work through difficulties and frustrations.

- Those who develop a reverence and respect for all things will walk lightly on the earth and will know peace.

- The less often we think of ourselves and the more often we think of others, the more we will understand their point of view, the better our relationships will be and the more friends we will have.

- Those who act superior and prideful are usually attempting to mask feelings of inferiority. Understanding this can help us to communicate with sympathy and perhaps learn to know another's strengths as well as weaknesses.

- Cutting down others in an attempt to make ourselves appear better rarely increases our popularity, and usually results in hurt, insecurity and dislike.

- If we wish to develop our own ability and creativity, we need to stop asking others to do what we can do for ourselves. This includes asking for advice which we then likely will not want to act on.

- A subconscious pattern that we may need to explore is the tendency to set ourselves up as a target for gossip and criticism, thereby unconsciously justifying hurt feelings and low self-esteem.

- We need to be careful not to inflict our moods on others.

- Good manners oil the wheels of human relationships.

- Being considerate of others pays big dividends.

- Couples who bicker in front of others, or talk too much about how wonderful their relationship is, make people uncomfortable, and leads to suspicion that they are putting on a front.

Affirmations for Loving Others

- We are all children of the One, unique and important to the universal plan.

- The Creator loves each of us equally. I am one with and express this universal, unconditional Love.

- I love and respect everyone as a child of God; or, I am learning to love and respect everyone as a child of God.

- I help those who ask for my assistance when I am sure that they truly need my help.

- I love others because I love myself.

- I acknowledge and respect the needs of others.

- I feel compassion for the plight of others, knowing that life can be difficult.

- I reach out to others to cultivate the bonds of friendship.

- I include others in my joy.

- I give freely to others without measuring what is returned.

- In loving others I am loving myself.

- I am exactly where I need to be. I have drawn to myself the people and environment I need for the next step in my growth.

- I am calm and centered, no matter what is said about me.

- I am open to the opinions of others, but never overwhelmed by them.

- I will please myself today as well as doing things to please others.

- I am responsible for changing and improving myself, not others.

- I release myself from the need to control others or to allow them to control me.

- I claim my own power by detaching from the expectations and demands of others and peacefully choosing the course of action that is right for me.

- God has created each one of us as a special and unique flower in the garden of life. I enjoy this fascinating garden and am doing my part to keep it beautiful.

Meditations for Loving Others

Exercise 1

Close your eyes. Visualize a person with whom you are having difficulty. Picture that person standing before you as clearly as you can. Meet his or her gaze and look deeply into his or her eyes.

Now see the White Light of Universal Love surrounding this person. Watch the White Light vibrating and entering every cell of his or her being.

Now notice that the White Light is also surrounding and entering you. See yourself and the other saturated with the same lovely vibrant light. Feel that both of you are glowing and being healed of the difficulty. Then ask your inner source for the wisdom to bring about what you have just seen.

Exercise 2

Again visualize the person with whom you are having conflict. See that person before you and note that he or she, too, is hurting inside because of your differences. You are surprised and relieved to see these emotions that have been unexpressed. Compassion begins to well up in your heart when you realize that the other one is also upset and suffering.

Picture a ball of white light flowing from your heart to the other's heart. See the other person smiling and happy in the light of your love and forgiveness. See light from the other person's heart coming back to bless you.

In the light, picture all conflicts dissolved. Know that you can find a way to bring this about.

Exercise 3

Visualize yourself standing at the edge of a quiet forest. In front of you is the serene and peaceful ocean. On the horizon is a glorious rainbow.

Bring the colors streaming from the rainbow one by one in to saturate your being. The red fills you with strength and vitality. The orange charges you with confidence and enthusiasm. Yellow brings joy and mental power. The glory of green offers love, health and harmony. Blue lifts you with creativity and devotion. Indigo magnetizes you with intuition.

Violet transforms you with creative imagination, humility and spiritual understanding.

Now see yourself with others around you. Picture the colors and their corresponding qualities as an endless supply flowing from your heart to your associates. See everyone around you receiving these uplifting vibrations which transform them. Give thanks.

Exercise 4

Picture yourself in a beautiful and fragrant garden. Everything is perfect and in harmony. See all your loved ones in this garden of tranquility. They are smiling with love.

Now visualize the whole world as being a garden. See all the inhabitants of planet Earth happy and living in peace. Because thoughts and pictures have power, you are helping to bring about peace and good will.

THE LOVE OF GOD

In Love with Love

In love there are three elements: the lover, love itself, and the beloved. In various relationships it is the beloved that helps each of us open our heart, but ultimately it is the feeling of love in our own heart that we cherish. The love of God is born with this realization: *God is Love and Love is God.*

We can unite with our Creator by learning to quiet our thoughts and concentrate on the love in our heart. In this we become united with all things. Once having had direct experience of God, our natural wish is to encourage other souls to discover their own oneness with Universal Love. We then desire to give unconditionally of our time and energy to work for the will of Love, first in our own life and then with others.

Desire for God

The following section contains inspirational thoughts to encourage us to develop a desire for Spiritual growth. Once the desire is established, our yearning for union with our Creator begins to grow. When we seek Universal Love with intensity and consistency, that yearning draws a response from God.

Again, I would like to emphasize that God is neither masculine nor feminine, although the Creator may display any aspect that is dear to the Spiritual seeker. In using the following ideas and exercises, please feel free to change the gender or particular manifestation mentioned to suit what is sacred to you.

Love Is the Source of Our Being

God as Love is our Creator and Sustainer. Everything that we hold dear is an expression of Love's creative intelligence. All power to think, breathe and live comes from Cosmic Love. Without Infinite Spirit all creation, including our own being, would cease to exist.

We Are Conceived in Love

God made each one of us as a special act of creation. He took a unique interest in us, and is constantly watching over us, aware of our every thought and feeling, without judgement. We can affirm that our Creator loves us so much that He focused His Infinite Love on creating us.

Love Created Us in Its Image

We are told that the Supreme Source is everything - the All in All. When Divine Consciousness created, It used Its own essence, for there is nothing outside of Spirit. We are formed out of Love. Love holds all creation together.

God as Our Divine Parent

We are not manufactured objects thrown into the sea of space and left to fend for ourselves. We are Love's offspring made in Its essence. Universal Love is guiding and sustaining us at every moment if we are open to accept it. In a personal sense, the Creator is our Heavenly Father and Divine Mother and we all are children of the Most High.

God Is Our Perfect Father

In the Father aspect of Spirit, God protects and sustains us throughout eternity. He guides and lets us experience to help us to grow in His image.

God Is Our Perfect Mother

Universal Love expresses Itself in the form of the Divine Mother, the feminine aspect of God. She gives birth to us, showers us with unconditional love, and forgives and comforts us no matter what we may have done.

God as Our Perfect Friend

We can talk to God as our closest friend, knowing that Spirit understands and loves us as no one else can. God is our constant companion with whom we can safely share all our life's experiences.

God as Our Beloved

As the lover thinks constantly of the beloved, so the Spiritual man yearns for God. As the Divine Beloved, God is the only One that can lastingly fulfil and satisfy our hearts and needs.

We Are Heirs to the Entire Universe

All things are vibrating in the sea of Universal Love. In our oneness with Spirit, we contain the imprint and potential of everything that exists.

Spirit Has Given Us Infinite Divine Qualities

We are changeless, immortal souls. Our nature is love, peace, power, joy, wisdom, compassion, confidence, strength and vitality. We do not have to acquire these, for they are already within us. Our purpose is to uncover them and allow them to shine forth.

Each Soul Has Unique and Special Gifts

No two grains of sand are exactly alike. Each person is an individualized expression of Infinite Spirit. We are here to fully manifest our own special gifts and talents.

God Has No Favorites

Universal love shares Its love equally and unconditionally with all. God knows that each soul is at a different stage of evolution, and that all are Saints in the making. God has a unique personal relationship with each of His children; all are special.

God Has Given Each of Us Free Will

We have been given the priceless gifts of reason and free will so that we can choose and experience whatever we want. In our essence we are dynamic beings, not puppets of destiny. We have the potential to mold our lives in any way we wish. We have even been given the freedom to accept or reject the very Source of our being and the things that are our birthright.

Love's Many Blessings

We each have been blessed with a mind and body with which to live in the outer world which was created for our enjoyment. God has given us the beauty of nature which is there to envelop and enrich our lives. We have all been given material possessions to use and enjoy. Divine Love has given us our loved ones so that we may help one another. For these and many other blessings our Higher Power deserves our heartfelt gratitude.

We Receive According to Our Receptivity

Never does our Creator weary of giving from His boundless treasures, nor can Love's mercies be exhausted. Every effort we make to know our infinite nature and to do good in this world will bring a reward. Yet nothing is forced upon us. Unconsciously we make choices that bring to us what we experience.

All our prayer-demands are heard. We do not always get what we ask for or what we might like, but we each get what we truly need for the next step in our growth. Universal Love has already given us every blessing, and all we have to do is to make ourselves open to receive them. Too often we block our own good with our negativity and inability to accept what could be ours, or by our feelings of unworthiness.

God Yearns for Our Love

When we disconnect ourselves from our Creator we become separated from the Source of our being. In this separation not only are we incomplete, but so is Love. God yearns to receive our love as a free and spontaneous gift. By offering our love to our Creator, we help make the Eternal Heart whole again and therein find our own completeness.

God Is the Highest Necessity

Spirit not only created the universe with all its qualities, but our individual beings as well. With such a gift, it is not only wise but essential that we be on intimate terms with our Creator. Unfortunately, there are many in this world who not only fail to communicate with Spirit, but actively push God out of their lives. As a result the world finds itself in a state of Spiritual bankruptcy.

There are many reasons why people in general are afraid to meet and embrace their Maker. In their early religious training, people have been erroneously taught that God is a vengeful old man waiting to punish them for the slightest transgression. This is a cruel misunderstanding, for God operates only out of love.

Universal laws are for our benefit to bring harmony into our lives. They afford order and cooperation among all things. If universal laws did not exist, the cosmos would be in a state of chaos. Laws such as the Bible's ten commandments are equal and exact for everyone. We have been given reason and conscience to let us know if we are in or out of harmony with these laws.

As an act of love, our Creator has given us free will. We are free to choose whatever we wish. If we go against these guidelines for happiness, then we go against our highest good. It is the impartial justice of universal laws that lets us know when we are in error, because we suffer the consequences in pain and unhappiness.

Our concept of God is unconsciously largely drawn from our relationship with our parents. Our attitudes towards the "Heavenly Father" or "Divine Mother" are strongly conditioned by our early feelings towards these earthly counterparts.

Another factor that leads us astray is the overemphasis that has been put on material life. Almost everyone is preoccupied with making money. Many people reason: "Who has time for God in all this madness? I need to work, to keep myself and my family together, and hopefully to have some time to relax."

But God is the only sanity in all this chaos. *Our Creator is the only constant in a universe of flux, the only real refuge, the only true prosperity.* Even if we acquire a billion dollars, if we have not made the acquaintance of Spirit, in the eyes of Infinite Wisdom we are penniless, and in our hearts we are poor.

This world of form is a play of opposites, and reverses are inevitable. Penniless is how we come into this world, and penniless is how we go out. The only thing we can take with us is the love and wisdom we have awakened within ourselves. While our earth visa is still valid, it is paramount that we spend some time every day acquiring lasting values, developing ourselves, and being considerate of others. Above all, we need to spend time making contact with our Creator who sustains us at every moment, and who will continue to do so for eternity.

Although many are convinced that seeking Universal Love is not very practical, Spirit nevertheless takes care of Its own. Christ said: "Seek ye first the kingdom of God and His righteousness and all these things will be added unto you." The Creator always works for our highest and best interest. I remember one Saint saying that Divine Mother will definitely make sure you have a roof over your head if you are seeking Her with complete sincerity, and outwardly working to please Her.

Many people feel that the Divine is not really interested in their personal wants and desires, and that if they turn to their Creator, they will have to give up all their pleasures and material happiness. God is not trying to sabotage us. In fact, the Creator is deeply interested in our happiness and our ultimate well-being. Spirit created this world and us and understands our needs and desires.

God is on Our Side

If we experience any lack in our life, it does not follow that God is punishing us. The fault lies with something in our own consciousness. If, for example, we do not have enough money to fulfil our responsibilities and desires, it is not our Creator who is preventing us from attaining these, but some conscious or subconscious kink in our own minds and the way we do things.

We may consciously or unconsciously hold the limiting thought that money is unspiritual. We may even believe that we need to embrace poverty to be pleasing to God. This is not necessarily true. Many Saints cautioned against the acquisition of money because people tend to place money on the altar of their hearts, making it their God and forgetting the Eternal One who is the supreme treasure and security.

Every Saintly soul, however, has used money in one form or another. Lazarus helped Jesus with his material needs and contributed generously to his Savior's mission. God is practical and down to earth. He has created rain so seeds can grow. God has placed intelligent life-force in our stomachs to help digest our food. Our Creator knows our needs and desires, and is sympathetic to our wants. But He gave us free will and nothing is forced on us.

The Goal Is Love

The universe, with all its complexity and challenge is, in essence, relatively simple. It is Spirit's cosmic dream, God's super-colossal movie theater. The plot of the Divine drama is this: *the Supreme One who created us is seeking our love.* Spirit has everything, all knowledge, power and bliss. As the Creator of all, there is nothing God does not own. The only gift that we can offer that will touch the Divine Heart is our love. Our Creator wants us to give that love as a spontaneous and willing gift. God, in generosity, has given us the priceless gift of free will and we can choose to give our allegiance to our Creator or to the world. Unfortunately, the majority of mankind chooses the world, and thus finds suffering on almost every level of life.

Universal Love has infinite patience. Our Creator silently waits for us, for He knows that no matter what worldly goal we seek, we will eventually become frustrated and disappointed. We will find that nothing can satisfy the heart but Love alone. No amount of money or material possessions, nor even human love and friendship, can fill the emptiness of the heart that we experience due to separation from our Creator.

Peter asked Jesus, "Where else can we go?" When we mature spiritually, we find there is nowhere else to turn. Reflect on the love you feel in your heart for the individual who is the dearest to you. Get a sense of this love. Now take the fullness of this love and multiply it a million times. Imagine how overwhelming this love would be. Even the magnitude of this love cannot compare with the satisfaction and contentment the soul feels when united with God.

In trying to convey the intensity of this love, a Saint once described it as feeling the love of a million mothers in one's heart. Remember that God, as the Divine Mother, is the sum total of all love, the love of all the lovers who have ever loved.

How to Cultivate Love for God

Developing a Personal Relationship

How can we capture this love? We need to ask God for it. Many say, "Yes, I do pray, but I get no response." Our Creator does listen, and responds if our prayers are sincere. We just don't recognize what that response is. If, however, we offer God just a passing thought such as, "Hi, Lord, I want your love. Send me some money. Good night, Lord." That attitude will never bring us the love we seek. That attitude will not even work in the world. Imagine what you would think if someone approached you with that kind of request.

To get results you have to get down to business with God. You need to know how the Divine operates. To get a response from God, you need to satisfy the requirements of the law and also offer your heart-felt love.

So, what is a procedure we can follow in order to make ourselves receptive to Spirit? The first step is to develop a tangible, personal relationship with Infinite Love. We need a workable concept that we can relate to in every moment of life. In order to have an intimate relationship with our Creator, it is helpful to have an inner representation of an image or form that we can visualize, and to whom we can direct our prayers and our love.

We all need someone we can talk to, someone to whom we can pour out our hearts. God as Spirit is infinite, omnipresent, omniscient, and all-powerful; however, it is very difficult for most people to pour their hearts out to infinite omnipresence or to feel that omniscience is their constant companion throughout life. *We need to develop a relationship with an aspect of the Creator to which we can feel close and connected, and which will sustain us not only during our prayer time, but in every other phase of our life as well.*

This personal relationship can be nurtured by visualizing God in whatever form most inspires our appreciation and feelings of gratitude and love. It can be perceived as a brilliant and glorious White Light, or may take on a more personal aspect such as the Heavenly Father, or Divine Mother. One may wish to dwell on a great soul such as Jesus, or any one of God's great saints.

Simple Techniques for Spiritual Awareness

A mental image is not idolatry, but a symbolic representation of the actual presence of Spirit. It makes Universal Love more tangible and accessible. The symbolic form gives us a concrete focus for our energy and love. Visualizing our chosen form can make it easier for us to talk to God. For some, it is helpful to use a picture. By repeatedly looking at the picture and then closing the eyes, one can gradually develop or strengthen the power of visualization.

The Spiritual eye, or third eye, is the door to the superconscious state and by visualizing a chosen form there, it is easier to tune into Spiritual states of consciousness. Jesus spoke of the Spiritual eye when he said, "If thine eye be single, thy whole body will be full of light." At death, the consciousness of man is usually drawn to this sacred center, accounting for the upraised eyes found in those close to death.

The Spiritual eye is located between the eyebrows above the bridge of the nose. You can focus your attention at this point and gently upturn your eyes towards this center. If you feel any strain or it feels like you are becoming "cross-eyed" then you need to soften your focus. When practiced correctly, this technique will give you a tremendous feeling of peace. You may eventually feel a soothing pulsating energy accumulating at this point, or see a light or colors.

The practice of concentration on the spiritual eye may take some time to perfect but it is well worth the effort. It is useful to practice for a short time in the beginning, and gradually increase the time as you feel more comfortable. If you feel a strain, you can simply visualize your chosen image within. Be careful not to allow your eyes to drift downwards, or you are likely to fall into a subconscious state, or even to sleep. This technique can be practiced often for short periods of time until you feel comfortable keeping the gaze continually at the Spiritual eye and offering your love.

The heart is the feeling center where we are able to feel a response from God. So, with mind and emotions calm, and with attention fixed either at the spiritual eye or at the heart, we can send our prayer-requests and love to the Creator, and receive a response in return.

Spirit, with all Its Divine qualities, is within us at the core of our being and can be perceived at these Spiritual centers. Saint Augustine spoke of this when he said that he had wrongly sought and could not find the Lord without, for He was all the time within himself.

Another useful practice may be to meditate on the life of a Spiritual master, inwardly visualizing an event from that individual's life. By imagining ourselves in that particular scene as well, we can feel we are sharing the experience and absorbing the Spiritual vibrations. We can also come to feel that this Spiritual presence is with us throughout the day. By being creative we can find whatever works for us personally. The idea is to choose and practice whatever inspires our devotion.

Personal Manifestations of God

Jesus approached God as the Infinite Father, but the Christian world is instead mainly devoted to the form of Jesus. Because we are creatures in form, it is much easier to relate to the form of Jesus than it is to similarly devote oneself to an abstract concept such as the Omnipresent Father-aspect of Spirit. For example, one of Saint Francis' favorite meditations was to imagine that he was lovingly and tenderly taking Jesus down from the cross, and looking after the body of his Lord.

We can take whatever human relationships we cherish the most and transfer these feelings to the Creator. For example, if we feel a special love for our earthly mother or father, or if we are missing that relationship in our life, then we can make God our Divine Mother or Heavenly Father. If friendship is special to us, we can be with God, the best of friends. We can form a relationship in which God is the Master and we are the servant. God can also become the Beloved. If we feel a strong love for children, then the Creator can be the Divine Child.

Saint Anthony of Padua was inclined towards a fatherly love. This was the kind of love to which he could most easily relate. He became devoted to Christ in the form of baby Jesus. He imagined that the form of the baby Jesus was in his arms and he was lovingly taking care of Him. In time Christ did appear to him as the baby Jesus.

One Christian man who was having a great deal of difficulty in his life approached his minister for help and prayers. The minister suggested he take all his problems directly to Jesus. In order to do this, the minister asked the man to set up two chairs in a special spot: one chair would be for himself, and the other would be for Jesus. The man was then counseled to visualize Jesus in the other chair, and to direct all his problems and questions to Him. In the beginning of this communication process, he was simply to think of what Jesus might say in response to his questions. By following this process he found answers to all his questions.

The daughter of this man reported a beautiful story regarding his death. She was with him just before his passing, but had to leave the room for a few moments. Upon her return, she found him dead, and was extremely surprised to see her father's head resting on the chair beside the bed with a beatific smile on his face. She related her findings to the minister, who intuitively knew what had happened, for this was the chair that the man had dedicated to Jesus.

Many masters of India have achieved liberation through worshipping God in the form of the Divine Mother. Paramahansa Yogananda and Sri Ramakrishna have said that the form of the Divine Mother constantly appeared to them, and ultimately merged their consciousness in the Cosmic Father as well.

Saint Thérèse of Lisieux told of a healing she received through the Virgin Mary. Finding no earthly aid for a serious and distressing illness, Thérèse turned to a statue of her Heavenly Mother and entreated Mary with all her heart to have pity upon her. The face of the statue assumed an expression of ineffable kindness and compassion, and smiled at Thérèse. At once she felt her pains vanish, and she was instantly filled with pure, heavenly joy.

Saint Theresa of Avila, the great Christian mystic, tells us that her greatest meditation was to picture Christ inwardly, and if she thought of any incident of His life she would imagine it inside herself. She tells us that she particularly liked to visualize Jesus when he was alone, afflicted, and in need. She said that when she saw Christ this way she found it easier to approach Him. Even as a child she would visualize Jesus in the garden of Gethsemane on the night of his decision to follow the will of the Father and hand Himself over to the Pharisees. In her mind she would go and keep Him company, and attempt to comfort Him. She tells us that she received many blessings from this practice.

Saint Theresa also suggests that we take our chosen image within and speak to that form in the language of our hearts. She counsels us to give our love freely, spontaneously, and with ease. She mentions that we can ask for things that we are in need of, or outline difficulties or problems, and ask for comfort and strength to help us through the trials we are going through. We can share all our successes and joys as well as our difficulties.

Calmness and Stillness

In addition to establishing a personal relationship with the Creator, it is important to develop the qualities of stillness and calmness. In Psalms we read, *"Be still and know that I am God."* This can be expressed, "Be still and know yourself as the Soul, which is made in the image of God."

As long as the mind is restless and fickle, and the heart is continually agitated by likes and dislikes, we cannot fully perceive Spirit. Take a glass of muddy water and stir it up; when the water is agitated you cannot see anything reflected in it. As the water calms down, the mud will settle to the bottom of the glass. When the water is perfectly still the surface will reflect an image.

The same is true of the mind. As long as it is agitated with restlessness and permeated with thoughts of materialism, it cannot reflect the pure image of God. When it becomes still and the mud of worldly thoughts begins to settle down, a profound transformation takes place: the mind becomes the soul, or pure consciousness, and is able to mirror the pure image of Spirit within. By the power of intuition, our Creator can then be perceived or felt.

Most people do not practice this important first step, so their thought-prayers are ineffective, becoming lost in a myriad of other thoughts and distractions. Usually it is only when people are extremely desperate that they are able to forget all else and concentrate on God. By learning to calm the mind daily, we can offer our prayer-requests without waiting for some emergency to force us to seek allegiance with Universal Love.

Practicing the Presence of God

We can learn to continually communicate with our Creator throughout the day whenever we are not busy. Even at work, during break periods, we can let our thoughts rest in our chosen concept of God, rather than allowing our minds to fill with worries, hurt feelings, and resentments. We can reflect on how much our Creator loves us, and can offer loving thoughts in return.

Brother Lawrence described this continual mental attunement as "Practicing the presence of God." By disciplining himself in this way, he found that he was just as much with God in the kitchen amidst the pots and pans as he was when on his knees in the chapel. Brother Lawrence attested to his own unbroken communion which was peace, love and joy.

In addition to talking to the Creator, we can sing love songs to the Divine. We can take a song that has already been written to Spirit and make it our own. By concentrating on the meaning of the words and singing it from the heart, we can put our own sincerity and devotion into the song as our own special way of communing.

One beautiful thing we can do is to take a popular song we enjoy and change the words so we are singing to the

Divine. We can also make up our own original songs to God. The Divine Beloved appreciates every thought, every inspiration, and every act of love. It is marvelous what giving attention to our love for God will do for our own well-being and peace of mind.

Suggestions to Reestablish Love for God

- If you are not sure whether God really exists, sincerely ask to be shown the truth. If you are humble and earnest, your Creator will respond with an outward or inward sign that He is real, and that He cares.

- If you do not feel desire and yearning for God-realization, pray to the Divine Heart to help you experience God's love in your life. Prayer needs to be offered in intimacy and confidence with words spoken sincerely like a true child of God, not as a beggar. God does not glory in anyone's wallowing in unworthiness. We all have a legitimate right to our Divine heritage right here and now, and the Creator wants us to open to accept his bounty and love.

- The Creator can best be approached with the simplicity of a child. Love is very informal, and an intellectually programmed set of prayers spoken mechanically is surely as boring to God as it is to us. So pray in the language of your heart rather than repeating someone else's words.

- When we feel love welling up in our hearts for someone we love, we can remember that all love comes from God, and give thanks. In gratitude we can also direct this feeling of love towards the Creator.

- The best way to receive love is to give it. We need to offer our hearts to God, who wants our love. The Creator is the most generous of givers, and when we give our love, the response will be repaid a thousandfold.

- It can be helpful to take a passage from the Scriptures or other inspirational writings that is to us uplifting and encouraging. You can dwell on it and place it where it can be seen throughout the day. Think about it, try to understand its meaning and then seek to feel it in your heart.

- We can offer up our mistakes, no matter how severe they may seem. Divine Love does not judge. It wants to help us overcome whatever stands in the way of our growth and unfoldment. It knows that we learn through our mistakes.

- If we can accept and trust in Universal Love's concern for our well being in all circumstances, then we can learn to relax and accept what is coming to us no matter what the external conditions seem to be. When we are relaxed, we can be receptive to the presence of the Divine Consciousness within. God's guidance; peace and joy can then be felt in our consciousness.

- Supreme Intelligence is the power behind the universe. When we tune in to this power, we can be in tune with Its will; then we can experience God as the doer, working through us.

- We can perform all our activities as offerings to God. In eating, working, cleaning, and other daily responsibilities, we can feel we are doing these in a manner pleasing to God and of service to Him. Such a way of looking at what we do increases our devotion, and draws us closer to Divine Love.

- We can learn to evaluate our actions and the situations we encounter. Whatever leads us to the love of God can be embraced; whatever takes us away from it needs to be replaced.

- We can feel awe for the Supreme Intelligence that created the wonders of nature, in its subtle and mighty rhythms and infinite variety of forms. This lifts us above petty annoyances.

- If we truly want to feel our connection to Infinite Love, it is best to set aside a specific time each day when we can be alone and uninterrupted in seeking our communion.

- We can creatively place little reminders in our daily lives to help us remember to keep God in our thoughts. We can write something inspirational and put it on our desks to look at from time to time. We might set our clocks or watches to beep on the hour as a reminder to think of our Creator. These simple acts will soon fill our days with the consciousness of Divine Love.

Meditation

Meditation is an ancient science used in all Spiritual traditions seeking direct communion with God. In meditation the body and mind are stilled so that the subtle vibrations of Spirit can be perceived. Meditation is scientific because it yields a sequence of predictable results. Great souls declare that Spirit is beyond motion, and can only be known in the silence. *Meditation enables us to enter into deeper levels of silence, where we have actual perceptions and proof of the existence of God.*

Deep breathing exercises are often used before meditation proper, because they help to oxygenate the body and clear much of the carbon dioxide and other metabolic wastes from the system, allowing our breathing and our minds to become calm and still. Physical exercises such as Hatha Yoga relax the muscles to help prepare the body for deep meditation.

One of the most effective meditation techniques is to simply watch the breath flowing in and out, in and out. Many have achieved God-realization through this one technique alone, which has been practiced for millenniums in India.

If you wish to practice this technique, do not force your breath in any way, or try to control it. Simply observe it flowing in and out of the nose and the lungs. You can also follow the rise and fall of your chest. Watch your breath with as much detachment as possible as if watching someone else breathe. Watching it in this way, causes it to calm down of itself. When the breath becomes calm, the mind also slows down and the thoughts can be stilled. A still mind is like a flawless mirror which reflects the Infinite Self within.

To make this process more effective, you can repeat a word or phrase when the breath flows in, and another word or phrase when the breath flows out. In the book, The Way of a Pilgrim, a Russian peasant practiced the presence of God by continually repeating the Jesus prayer, "Lord Jesus Christ, have mercy on me" throughout the day. In time his subconscious mind took up the practice and he would awaken from sleep to find himself still inwardly repeating the prayer.

This Saintly man achieved tremendous Spiritual stature by constantly repeating this "prayer of the heart." He eventually learned to repeat the Jesus prayer in rhythm with his breath. On the ingoing breath he mentally whispered, "Lord Jesus Christ...," and on the outgoing breath he silently repeated, "...Have mercy on me." Thus he was continually chanting the Jesus Prayer with every breath.

Anthony de Mello, a greatly respected Jesuit priest, suggested that we repeat "Je..." on the ingoing breath and "...sus" on the outgoing breath. With each cycle of breath he thus repeated with devotion the name of Jesus. Instead of using the name "Jesus" we can substitute another name or a simple phrase which satisfies our hearts.

Tremendous spiritual power, grace, and fulfillment can be attained by the practice of this simple technique.   It can quickly bring God into our lives and lead us beyond delusion.

Manifestations of Spirit

Light

How does our Creator respond to us? The Omnipresent Spirit usually manifests as light, sound, intuition, or a feeling in the heart. It is important to remember that Cosmic Light and Sound are perceived through the inner or Spiritual senses, and not the ordinary physical way of perceiving. These senses operate through our astral, or energy body. Just like our physical body, the astral body has a definite anatomy consisting in part of seven chakras, or Spiritual centers along the spine. We experience God as light and sound through the faculty of intuition working through these inner senses. Ramakrishna spoke of these astral senses by beautifully describing them as our "love ears and love eyes," and our astral body as our "love body."

Jesus said, "If thine eye be single, thy whole body shall be full of light." This describes the manifestation of the Heavenly Father as light in the Spiritual eye. When we focus on the White Light in the Spiritual eye it eventually expands and fills the entire body. As we continue to expand with this light and merge with it, we can realize that our consciousness is present throughout the Universe.

Put dye in water and what happens? It spreads out and takes on the dimensions of the container. The same is true with our consciousness. Once connected with the Infinite Spirit of God, our consciousness spreads to encompass the Universe, and we become united with all created things.

In the Spiritual eye we can occasionally see visions, or the colors of the individual chakras: red for the Coccygeal or Basal center or chakra, orange for the Sacral, yellow for the Lumbar or Solar Plexus, green for the Dorsal or Heart, blue for the Cervical or Throat, indigo for the Spiritual Eye, and violet and white light for the Crown Chakra or Thousand-Petaled Lotus.

Sound

God also manifests as the Cosmic Sound of Amen, the Aum or the Om of the Hindus, which represents what the Bible calls the Word, Comforter, and Holy Ghost. The first experience of this cosmic sound comes within and then expands to infinity. Just as with color, each chakra has a corresponding sound which can be intuitively perceived in deep meditation.

St. John referred to these chakra centers as the seven churches, candlesticks, stars, and seals. He mentioned one of the chakra sounds when he talked of harpers harping with their harps. (Revelation 14:2) The astral harp sound is one of the chakra sounds. St. John also described the cosmic sound as the voice of many waters. When we hear the Holy Ghost or Om sound, it resembles the ocean roar, the cosmic motor of the universe. It can also take the form of words in our native language and give us precise guidance and reassurance. St. John of the Cross called this sacred sound the sonorous sound, or sonorous river.

Intuition and Form

At first the Creator seldom speaks to us openly, but responds to us and guides us through our intuition. *Feeling this intuitive guidance within us is one of the greatest proofs of God's presence.* Mahatma Gandhi said that he never had any great revelations, but simply learned how to follow the voice within.

In time, as one's devotion becomes purified, Universal Love may appear in form and talk directly to the seeking one.

Jesus often appeared at night to St. Francis and conversed with him. As mentioned before, Ramakrishna and Paramahansa Yogananda frequently had direct conversation with the Divine Mother of the Universe. Moses talked with God "...as a friend speaketh unto a friend."

Regarding visions, Saints and Sages of every religion have cautioned us not to become too enamored of miracles, visions, and other phenomena. We may receive visions from time to time, offering us inspiration and direction to guide us on our way. If they come, accept them with gratitude, but do not look for flashing lights or flaming letters of gold. For one thing, they may not be true Spiritual experiences, but instead are likely to be subconscious projections or other forms that may be hallucination.

Some seekers think that if they trip and fall, it must be a special sign implying a particular direction they should take in their lives.   It more likely means they should watch where they place their feet. Continually asking for miracles is demanding that God constantly prove Himself. Our Creator does, on occasion, use miracles and visions, but would much rather draw us to Him through love.

Feeling

We can experience the comforting presence of God as a feeling of deep peace, "The peace that passeth all understanding." Within this feeling of peace we can experience unfathomable love and joy.

Love is a beautiful and all-satisfying expression of God's presence. The whole world sings about romantic human love. In the physical expression of human love, such as kissing, it is the feeling of bonding, closeness and intimacy that really moves us. It is the sweet and tender feeling of love that we cherish.

In loving others, we are really seeking the feeling of love in our own hearts. The object of our love is the key that helps open our hearts to the love that is already there. Without the feeling of love that wells up from within ourselves, our relationships would be meaningless.

But what if we learn to open our hearts to love without depending on others? This is exactly what the Saints do; they go directly to God, and fall in love with Love itself. Love alone is the object of their love. This is why spiritual masters are sufficient unto themselves. Filled to overflowing with the love of God, they do not try to win the personal love of others, but instead allow their abundance to flow to the hearts of all.

Love is constant, unending, undying, and when we put our attention on love alone, we can never be disappointed, jilted or forsaken. Universal Love is not fickle or changeable, nor can it be snatched away by death. Love simply loves, and is unconditional. God is love, and love is God.

If we experience pure love bubbling up from within ourselves, and blend with this feeling of love, then we are in essence making love to God. Once again I would like to emphasize that by going directly to the source of love itself, great masters are living in the love of God all the time. In their actions Saints are working only for what they consider the Beloved. During prayer, they have intimate conversation with the Source of their heart's love. When they meditate in the stillness, they lose themselves in the wonder of love. Absorbed in the fullness of this love, they come to realize that they are one with Love itself.

Saints and Sages of all religions declare that the greatest perception of the Infinite is Joy, or Bliss. In the Hindu scriptures we read that the true nature of Spirit is Ever-Conscious, Ever-Existing, Ever-New Joy. Love is like the burning power of Divine fire, but the fire itself is Bliss. When we feel this overwhelming joy, or ecstasy, we know that we are in intimate contact with our Creator. *The bliss felt in deep meditation is the most convincing proof of the existence of God.* The cumulative effect of a lifetime of sense pleasures pales in comparison with the Bliss of God.

Affirmations for Loving Our Creator

- I am in God and God is in me.

- I acknowledge the God within me.

- I trust that my Creator will satisfy all the beneficial desires of my heart in His own time and in His own way.

- My Heavenly Father and Divine Mother are guiding and comforting me along the path of life.

- I walk in gratitude along the path of love.

- I will allow Divine Love to lead the way.

- Good flows into my life when I relax and let go and let Infinite Love take charge.

- God's Unconditional Love is my strength.

- Love has given Itself completely to me.

- I exist for eternity, I am loved for eternity.

- I live, move, and have my being in God's love.

- I am surrounded and filled with the love of God.

- I am eternally sustained by the Creator's love.

- I am safe in God's love.

Meditations for Loving Our Creator

Exercise 1

Close your eyes and picture the light of Universal Love come into your forehead. Watch it expand to fill and surround your entire head and move down into your body. Now see the light aglow in your heart. Love's light expands and soon your entire body and mind are bathed in Its radiance. Now feel that light saturating your every cell with love. Imagine yourself melting into the light. Continue to expand with Universal Love and Light. Merge with the light as it gradually spreads out to fill and bless all space, everywhere.

Exercise 2

Place two chairs facing each other in a special spot. Sit on one of the chairs and imagine that Jesus, or another Spiritual master, is sitting on the other chair. If you have chosen Jesus you may picture what Christ looked like or how you imagine He might look if He were with you. If you do not easily visualize, just get a sense of His presence in the chair.

Now pour out your heart to your chosen person. Say whatever you feel, including any doubts you may have. If you feel you have made major mistakes, share them. If you feel love and yearning for the Spiritual master, offer this to him or her now. If you cannot find anything to say, then share the events of your day. Then still your mind and give Spirit a chance to communicate with you.

In this visualization it is extremely important that one take the time to listen to the response. True communication flows both ways. One speaks to a Loving God and He or She responds. If you do not seem to hear a response, then imagine what you think the Spiritual master would say. As you continue in this practice, Spirit will use your intuition to guide you. This is a very powerful method to become receptive to the will of Infinite Love.

Exercise 3

Visualize Infinite Love as the Divine Mother of the Universe. Notice Her lovely and compassionate face glowing with beauty, and tranquility. The Holy Mother is looking at you with eyes filled with infinite tenderness and love.

She motions you to come closer, and as you do, you feel surrounded with Her loving presence. The Divine Mother gently lifts you onto Her lap. Then she rests your head against Her heart and holds you close.

Never have you felt so safe and secure. As you rest in her warm embrace you know you are loved eternally and unconditionally. She softly assures you that her guidance and protection will be with you all the days of your life. Now let the Holy Mother know of your gratitude and love.

Exercise 4

Take a moment to think about the things that happened yesterday or today. Imagine you are reviewing the happenings as you would a movie passing before your inner sight. Go back and relive your experiences. Now repeat this process once again only this time, make sure you are in the movie, looking out through your own eyes. Start at the beginning, when you wake up in the morning. See your Spiritual master at your side as you go through the events of the day. Even as you brush your teeth and comb your hair, your teacher is with you, listening to your thoughts, willing to offer love and encouragement. Visualize this master sharing all your experiences such as eating, working, driving your car, and relating to your family, coworkers, or friends. During happy moments, notice that your teacher rejoices with you.

When you are sad, your Spiritual master offers sympathy and love. Imagine how it would feel to have this loving Spiritual presence always by your side. You can have it if you ask and attune to it.

Exercise 5

If you have already formed a personal relationship with God, then visualize that image now. Look into that Spiritual being's calm eyes and feel wisdom flowing from them into your own. Take these impressions into your mind and heart and dwell on them. Your personalized manifestation of God now projects a healing current from its Spiritual eye which alters your state of consciousness. Feel the powerful current entering your brain cells transforming life-diminishing thoughts and habit patterns into life-enriching ones.

Now visualize a ray of light emerging from this Being's heart and filling your own. Love fills your being. Notice how these holy vibrations heal you of pains and disappointments that have built up over your lifetime. Feel yourself being charged and magnetically alive. Rest for a time and enjoy this love.

After a while see both of you looking deeply into each others' eyes exchanging waves of love and understanding. You are magnetically being drawn closer together in an embrace of Divine Love.

Exercise 6

Visualize that which touches your own heart. Enlarge on it and feel it take over and expand through your whole being. Rest in that glow. Know that you can go back to this any time you want to.

Concluding Remarks

This book has been written as an inspirational guide to help prepare us for the basic questions which we will be asked in some form at the conclusion of our lives: How much did we love, and what did we learn?

Three aspects of love have been discussed; self-love, love for others, and love for the Creator, or God as you perceive Him or Her to be. We have also explored problem areas that may have prevented you from opening to love. To help you overcome limitations and unfold your full potential, a variety of affirmations and guided meditations have been offered. The attributes relevant to each stage of life have been reviewed.

This book points the way to ideal states to work towards. Remember that developing and perfecting one's ability to love is a never-ending process that continues throughout life until we fully establish oneness with God. We need to be patient with ourselves and make the journey a joyous and uplifting one for it is the true journey of life. We are on the greatest adventure it is possible to embark on and each effort we make represents progress.

If we quietly ask for guidance our Creator will take our hand and lead us along the path of Love. When God leads and we follow, and do our part, success is assured.

Books by Alex Jones

Seven Mansions of Color offers inspirational and practical methods for the use of color in one's daily life. Learn to use the benefits of color to attract harmony and happiness. You can saturate your environment with joyous and positive energy to bring new vigor, health, peace, prosperity and spiritual realization. Topics include: color in the aura; healing properties of color; spiritual awareness through color; color meditation; color in your home and wardrobe; etc.

Creative Thought Remedies condenses timeless wisdom into an easy-to-understand visual form. By studying these introductions, affirmations and charts you will find how to channel your energies so that you may become successful in all your undertakings. Topics include: what promotes and what diminishes joyous living; success as a way of life; transforming undesirable habits; relationships; and preparation of one's own personalized thought-remedy chart.

Guided Meditations by Alex Jones

Peace Beyond Stress is a powerful relaxation tape to soothe the body and mind. Side 1 assists you to create a mental holiday where all is peaceful and serene. In this place of tranquility you will find it easy to practice the dynamic technique of tension and relaxation exercises, which soothe your muscles and harmonize your body. You feel increasing peace as stress and tensions melt away. Side 2 is a relaxation exercise for the mind. Use this visualization when the mind is restless and thoughts and emotions seem to race everywhere needing to be brought under control. With a steady mind and heart you can learn to focus your full attention on thoughts and goals that are important to you until success is achieved.

Angels of Color & Sound is a guided color meditation on the seven rays emanating from the seven chakras. By following the meditation, the seven rays of divine qualities (vitality, courage, joy, love, peace, intuition, and soul realization) are awakened. Side 2 contains solo piano compositions that bring tranquility to a restless mind. *"My students and I have found the tape extremely constructive for the induced states of relaxation and meditation." - Y. McKinley (Toronto Yoga Center). "When I hear Angels of Color & Sound I am transported to a healing dimension. The meditation and music are deeply touching, and even now as I think of them I feel the rich blessing they impart." - Allen Cohen (Author - The Dragon Doesn't Live Here Anymore)*

Music for Relaxation by Alex Jones

Kali's Dream - Joyful piano melodies ripple like cool mountain streams with moods changing colors like the seasons. These pure and crystal-clear solo piano compositions evoke a subtle and beautiful feeling which just isn't present in much music popular today. The notes express the creative playfulness and depth of Nature in a way which touches the peace and beauty within each listener. *"Your music is so beautiful that I will have it played over KAZU. Thanks again for the magical music." - Mike Schmitz (KAZU fm) Pacific Grove, Calif. "Kali's Dream is so pretty you can close your eyes for your own dream." - OP Music Magazine*

Forever - Original uplifting music written by Alex Jones and featuring the beautiful guitar playing of David White. The majestic guitar sounds are interlaced with a soothing piano and synthesizer which help you tap into your most cherished memories. The journey begins with full instrumental arrangements and then drifts into a magical solo guitar rendition, keeping the listener climbing upwards toward the happy ending - a guitar selection that is both electrifying and rhythmic. Surrender yourself to these rays of musical light which will flow, into your mind and heart, filling you with the joy of life. Let them inspire you to reach out for all your goals and dreams. *"I often play Alex's tapes for the patients and staff at the hospital where I work. It's soothing expansive tones help us to cope better with pain, fear and boredom. It is especially useful for potentially tense situations such as intensive care work with the terminally ill." - S. Silverman RN, VA*

Awake & Dreaming - Devotional in nature, these simple melodies soothe the ache from your soul with a mellow blend of piano and synthesizer. The nine cuts are like gentle lullabies that enfold you in loving peace. Especially good after a tiring day. *"Awake and Dreaming is soothing, relaxing, energizing and inspiring. We use this tape, and others by Alex, in our workshops; they never fail to draw strong, positive feedback from the participants." - J. Kramer (Silva Instructor) Toronto. "Keep your magnificent work up - it is the finest available. I did a guided exercise using Awake and Dreaming just before our final exam and the students raved about how it calmed them for the impending test." A. Tequis (Manchester Comm. College)*

Other titles are available and if you would like further information or a free catalogue, etc., please write:

Eastern Gate Publishing, Inc., (705) 932-3536
either   PO Box 7, Millbrook, Ontario L0A1G0 Canada
or   PO Box 1485, Front Royal, VA 22630 USA